The Church Idea Book
More Than 200 Ideas!

Shane M. Groth and John D. Schroeder

Abingdon Press

The Church Idea Book

93 94 95 96 97 98 99 00 01 02 — 11 10 9 8 7 6 5 4 3 2

This book is printed on recycled, acid-free paper.

ISBN 0-687-08162-9

MANUFACTURED IN THE UNITED STATES OF AMERICA

To my wife, Sue,
who believes in my ideas
S. G.

To Pastor Ron Prasek,
an innovative spiritual leader
J. S.

The Reverend Shane M. Groth is an editor for Augsburg Fortress
Publishers in the area of adult curriculum. He graduated from
Luther Northwestern Seminary in 1987 and served as Associate
Pastor for Central Lutheran Church in Elk River, Minnesota, for
three and a half years. He lives in Otsego, the newest town in
Minnesota, with his wife, Sue, and two boys, Andrew and Michael.
He enjoys golf, fishing, tennis, karate (currently holds a brown belt),
and working on the computer.

John D. Schroeder is proprietor of The Word Store, which provides
desktop publishing services and freelance writing to individuals and
businesses in Minneapolis, Minnesota. A former newspaper
reporter, he is a graduate of Moorhead State University, Moorhead,
Minnesota, and served for nine years as a magazine editor for a
human resource development publishing firm. John is a member of
Oak Grove Lutheran Church in Richfield, Minnesota and is editor
of the congregation's monthly newsletter, *The Messenger*.

CONTENTS

Expanded Articles

INTRODUCTION

What do you do with an idea? That's an important question because in this book you'll be faced with two hundred ideas that have been utilized in churches during the past decade. There are several actions you can take. Ideas can be considered, refined, rejected, implemented, shared with others, or used as thought-starters for better ideas. And that's only the beginning.

This book is designed to stimulate your creativity so that the gospel may be proclaimed in new and different ways. Too often we rely on familiar behavioral responses and courses of action rather than try anything new. Events continue to get promoted solely in the church bulletin and from the pulpit, when with just a bit more thought and preparation, fresh and innovative promotional techniques can be utilized to reach new audiences. You are better than you think at coming up with dynamic ideas, and this book can be your catalyst.

Before you begin, however, there are some ground rules. First, there are no bad ideas. Some of the ideas contained within this book may initially seem to have little merit, but every single idea contains the promise of becoming an exceptional one if you will use the idea for the purpose it is intended: as a thought-starter. Each idea represents one way out of many ways to respond to a challenge in ministry. Utilize your members and committees as resources for developing ideas toward their full potential. Ideas need to be shared in order to germinate.

And finally, keep our eyes, ears, and mind wide open as you explore the many options for empowering your ministry. God has blessed you and your church with the brains and resources to meet every challenge. Dare to be creative and open your ministry to the exciting new possibilities that God has for you—each beginning with an idea!

APPRECIATION

IDEA: Show appreciation with a video keepsake.

One church gives departing staff and longtime members a good-bye that lasts for years. They videotape comments, farewells, favorite moments, funniest remembrances, and other highlights given by friends, acquaintances, church members, and staff. On the day the person leaves, the video is played at a reception between services so that everyone can enjoy the exchange. It is then given to the person as a lasting reminder of their friendships at the church.

IDEA: Place thank-you cards in the pew racks.

Everyone likes to be appreciated and here's one way you can encourage members of your church to offer a word of thanks to other members. One church placed thank-you cards in the pew racks one Sunday as part of their Celebration of Service. The cards were intended to provide members with the opportunity to thank those in the church family who ministered to them in some way during the past year. Near the end of the service, a "collection" was taken of all the cards. The following week the cards were distributed to the members by the church staff.

IDEA: Give gift certificates redeemable for free church services.

For meaningful gifts that last, why not give something incorporated into the life of the church that goes beyond meeting a physical need? For example, gift certificates for free marital counseling could be given to couples celebrating their first wedding anniversary. Coupons for use toward a week at the church's summer camp or for a weekend retreat could be given as confirmation gifts. Gift certificates could also be given on birthdays or anniversaries toward purchasing books at the church's bookstore. Local Christian gift shops may also offer your church substantial discounts or free discount coupons to give away on special occasions.

IDEA: Offer a surprise of an unexpected service or kindness.

Doing the unexpected for strangers, friends, and members of your congregation can be a real day brightener. As a secular example, one gas station gave everyone free full service and a gift on the day of their anniversary. To translate this to your church, perhaps one Sunday you might remove the cup for coffee donations, put up a note saying that no donations are necessary, and offer free donuts. Or the youth of your church could wash cars at no cost during Sunday services. Perhaps every tenth person who buys a ticket for the annual church dinner could get a dollar discount. What can you do to surprise someone?

IDEA: Record on cassette tape the remarks of longtime members.

When the oldest member in a congregation died recently, his family was given a cassette tape from his church of an interview with him about how he felt about his church and his faith. He had belonged to the same church all his life and at the time of his death the congregation was celebrating their 100th anniversary. The tape was treasured by the family, who were glad that someone took the time to interview him. A tape is also a wonderful keepsake for the church to pass on to future members. Is there someone in your church who could interview longtime members? Remember, the interview could also be done on videotape as well as audio cassette.

IDEA: Create a "Praise Box" to hold notes of appreciation.

It has been said that the most powerful prayer is the recognition of good. One way to release this power is to construct a "Praise Box" for showing appreciation. All you need to do is to place a container, similar to a ballot box, in the church office. Members can write messages of appreciation to a person or a group within the church. Provide paper and pencils and forward replies to recipients.

IDEA: Honor a "Person of the Week" every Sunday during services.

One church selects a person every week to be given public recognition for contributing to the church. (You could also do this once a month.) The name is announced during Sunday services, a photograph of the person is displayed, and the coffee hour after the service is in his or her honor. Honoring a person on a regular basis also helps people get to know others, connecting names and faces.

IDEA: Offer a Recognition Sunday at your church.

Set aside one Sunday a year for people of your congregation to appreciate each other and to communicate what they like about the church. Use small group meetings or try a potluck dinner. Distribute certificates of appreciation for members to present to each other.

IDEA: Hold a formal "thank-you dinner" followed by a prize drawing in which all in attendance are thanked.

Here is a unique way to thank people for contributing to your ministry and to give them something in return. As members arrive for dinner, a ticket with their name is placed in a box for a later drawing. Following dinner, names are drawn and each person is thanked for their contribution to the church. The last several tickets drawn win door prizes in addition to being thanked. The most valuable gift goes to the last ticket drawn. Donations or ticket sales cover the cost of the prizes.

COMMUNICATION

IDEA: Utilize the communication power of a P.S.

Did you know that in a letter, the P.S. gets the highest readership? And the best P.S. is an intriguing, but incomplete statement that the reader can only understand by going back and reading the letter's text. You can use a P.S. on postcards and even on brochures and flyers.

IDEA: Create a "Make-A-Wish" card to facilitate communication.

Here's a way to increase communication between the staff and the members of your church. One church has "Make-A-Wish" cards along with the hymnals in the pews and encourages members to use the cards to voice a desire or wish. The card contains a checklist of wishes like these: I wish we would sing this hymn; I wish the pastor would call on me; I wish the church would pray for_____; I wish to join a Bible study; I wish to thank_____; I wish you would change_____; and so on. The card also has a place for comments. Once the member writes a message, it can be dropped in the offering plate.

IDEA: Use your hand to control people and gain order.

If you are running a meeting, teaching a class, or maintaining order at a gathering, start out by explaining that every time you raise your hand, the group is to be attentive and should stop talking. Practice this a few times with the group until the response is automatic. It can save your voice and your nerves, and it helps things go more smoothly.

IDEA: Communicate prayer requests through your answering machine.

Here's a way to unite members of your church in prayer all during the week. One church is using one of their telephones and an answering machine to facilitate prayer requests. When someone calls the special phone line, the message on the machine gives the prayer requests for the week and allows the caller to record a prayer request after listening to the message. The recording is updated daily and can communicate prayers efficiently to an entire congregation.

IDEA: Burst a balloon during a talk to make a point.

If you ever need a method to get people's attention and make a point—burst a balloon. Inflate one or more balloons prior to your presentation or sermon, and perhaps write a word on them (such as "myth"). After you have made your point in the presentation, burst the balloon with a pin. Another way is to have someone come forward from the audience and burst the balloon. It gets your point across in a graphic way.

IDEA: Illustrate that anything is possible using a single word.

As an illustration of achieving something that looks impossible, ask someone to arrange the letters in the two words, "new door," to make one word. Give them a chance to try and then write on the blackboard or flip chart O-n-e-W-o-r-d.

IDEA: Remind your members of the services and help available.

One church frequently lists the many services provided by the staff and members in its newsletter and in the Sunday bulletin. This list included: worship, weddings, funerals, tape ministry, food bank, pastoral counseling, Sunday school, Bible studies, support groups, and special events. These were all listed under the heading: "Have a question? Have a need? Here are some ways we can help." It is a nice reminder of the scope of services available to members and nonmembers, emphasizing opportunities for involvement.

IDEA: Have your next guest speaker introduced by the audience.

If you are looking for an unusual way to introduce a speaker at a special event, have the audience do it! Here's how it works: Prior to introducing the speaker, go out into the audience and give slips of paper containing one or two facts about the speaker to selected people. When it is time to introduce the speaker, suggest that the speaker is so well known that everybody in the audience knows something about him or her. You then go out into the audience and ask your pre-selected people what they know about your speaker. They repeat their one or two facts from memory so that it looks spontaneous. It's a way for the audience to join in welcoming your guest, and one that the speaker will appreciate and remember.

IDEA: Pool ideas and resources for summer activities.

Everyone in your church has ideas and many also know of resources that can be beneficial to others. Why not bring all these ideas and resources together at an "Idea Pool Party" at your church? Select a topic or need, for example: free summer activities for children, or ways to increase summer worship attendance. Hold an evening gathering that mixes business with pleasure. Generating ideas can be fun! List all the ideas or have someone take notes so that this great information is not lost. Decide as a group what ideas should be implemented.

IDEA: Keep members informed of other groups that use your church who welcome their participation.

Do your members know what's going on at church during the week and how they can become involved? Chances are they already know about weekly church-sponsored activities, but do they know about weekly events that are not church-sponsored? One church lists in the weekly bulletin all groups that use their church that welcome others. Let your people know that groups like Alcoholics Anonymous, a judo club, Boy Scouts, sewing groups, and others are there for them. Keep communicating opportunities!

IDEA: Hold regular "all-church meetings" with members.

One way to keep in touch with the feelings and desires of members is to meet with them on a regular basis. One church calls their gatherings an "all congregational family chat" to gain input, ideas, and thoughts from members. The meeting is facilitated so that all participants get a chance to speak and exchange opinions and information. Church meetings do not have to be held once a year or only in times of crisis. By talking together, the church family becomes more of a family.

IDEA: Create and implement a neighborhood newsletter.

If you want to get in touch with your neighbors and encourage them to participate in church activities, how about creating a simple neighborhood newsletter? Here are two possible formats: (1) Include news of the neighborhood in a special section of your monthly church newsletter—and be sure that people in the area get a copy of it. It could include family news, people moving, new jobs, and so on. (2) Create a one-page, eight-by-ten-inch letter addressed to local residents containing news from the neighborhood. It's a personal way to stay in touch!

IDEA: Use attention-getters in your printed materials.

You can increase the effectiveness of your printed materials by following these techniques: (1) Use two colors of ink; one for the text and another for headlines. Studies have shown that two-color design draws more readers; (2) Include a map. Maps make it easier for people to find your church; (3) Use photographs and illustrations of people rather than the outside of buildings. People find "people pictures" more interesting; (4) Use headlines with all capital letters sparingly. Upper and lowercase words are easier on the eyes; (5) Leave some open space.

COMMUNITY OF FAITH

IDEA: Gather prayer requests from area churches.

Before weekly staff meetings, why not remember another church in your prayers? Better yet, call a church in your community, tell them you would like to support them in their ministry, and ask if they have any special prayer requests.

IDEA: Adopt a struggling or new church as a mission partner.

Two Lutheran churches in Minnesota, one urban and one rural, have teamed up as partners in ministry. They support and encourage one another in many ways. For example, each Sunday the congregation of the rural church prays for four families by name from the urban church during Sunday services. During the year, members of both churches visit each other and the pastors participate in a pulpit exchange. Letters are regularly exchanged and published in congregational newsletters. This partnership assists in emphasizing what both have in common, and facilitates friendships between people who normally would never meet.

IDEA: Co-sponsor a community project with another church.

There are many benefits in teaming up with another church. You can double your attendance, double your volunteers, and cut your expenses in half. Both churches can also work on publicity. This is a great way of showing Christian unity in action.

IDEA: Create a legion of "angels" within your church.

There are angels in your midst. One church regularly prints a notice of thanks to anonymous "angels" within the congregation who clean up the church grounds without being asked or decide as a group to help some individual or organization within the community. To get your angels started on needed work, print some needs and invite people to do the work or service when they can or as needed. Perhaps some angel T-shirts might be contributed to spark service to people, the church, and the community.

COMPUTERS

IDEA: Use "DOS shells" to make computer use easier.

If you have a hard time dealing with the C> prompt, EDLIN commands, formatting, renaming, or creating and copying directories on your hard disk, help is just a software package away. Programs called "DOS shells" simplify daily tasks of disk and file management with straightforward commands, pull-down menus, mouse support, and visual graphics. Some even include a calculator, appointment scheduler, outliner, and a powerful back-up program, all for under $100.

IDEA: Instead of upgrading, consider an integrated software package.

When you outgrow your word processing program, instead of upgrading it, for about the same price or less you can buy an integrated software package that covers word processing, spreadsheet, database, and telecommunication tasks. Because the commands are similar from task to task, it takes less time to learn. Although these may not be adequate for large churches, they do a wonderful job with most letters, memos, invoices, and small budgets.

IDEA: Utilize a software edition of an electronic concordance.

Wouldn't it be nice to find any word or phrase in the Bible in less than two seconds? Now you can with the help of a computer and an electronic concordance. You can search automatically for key words, phrases, biblical books, or a combination of these with a few key strokes. The text can also be printed out or placed in a word processing document. Some allow you to search the Hebrew and Greek texts as well. Many packages come in a variety of translations.

IDEA: Look at what you're getting when buying a computer package.

When buying a computer system, packaged prices don't always reflect the cost of a complete system. Be suspicious of very low prices and make sure that the following have been accounted for in the price: monitor, a graphics card that's compatible with your computer, enough RAM memory for programs (640K minimum), disk drives, and parallel or serial ports as needed for peripherals. You might simply ask, "What will it cost to get this system up and running?"

IDEA: Rent a laser printer instead of buying one.

Laser printers are hard to beat for the clear, crisp copy they give to finished computer documents. But you don't need to spend $1,000 or more to receive the benefits! Many duplicating services rent laser printers for as low as 50¢ per page. All you need to do is follow these steps: First, find a copy center that rents laser printers and ask for the make and model of the printer that is compatible with your computer. Second, tell your word processing program that you now have the above laser printer (this is usually done by selecting printer drivers; check under "printer definitions" in your word processing manual). This fools the computer into using the fonts and type settings of the defined laser printer. Three, input your document and copy the finished file to a floppy disk. Four, bring the disk to the copy center and print out the document. You now have the benefits of a laser printer without the costs!

IDEA: Enter into the world of computers by reading a church computer magazine.

Is your church ready to get involved in the world of computers, but you simply don't know where to start? One place to begin could be with *CHURCH BYTES: The Church Computer Magazine*. It offers news, product reviews, tips, and "a little bit of everything for using computers at home and in the church." Though it is geared for IBM users, it also includes information for those who use Macintosh computers. The subscription rate is $18 for eight issues. For a free copy or more details, write: Neil Houk, 562 Brightleaf Square #9, 905 West Main St., Durham, NC 27701; or call: (919) 479-5242.

IDEA: Make it easy to back up information.

You can save time, money, and information by following these suggestions for backing up information on your computer. First, save your information regularly. Back up your data daily or weekly at a set time. Second, back up your work automatically using your existing software. Many word processing programs, for example, back up your work in fifteen-minute intervals without you entering a single command. Third, think about buying a program specifically designed for backing up data. Most are inexpensive ($10-$75) and easy to use.

EVANGELISM

IDEA: Help members share the gospel through their talents.

While many churches use time and talent sheets to accomplish church-related ministries, what about using the same for those outside of the church? For example, one church asked member volunteers to supply labor for car repairs to those who could not otherwise afford them. (This included people in between jobs, those who just moved to the community, people with illness, and so on.) The "clients," who have no affiliation with the church, are referred by the pastor and pay for their own parts. The church volunteer is able to befriend someone in a significant way while sharing the gospel message through their gifts.

IDEA: Offer a midday break concert at your church.

During summer, one church invites members, friends, and neighborhood residents to drop in with a brown-bag lunch and hear an organ recital. They offer several one-hour mini-concerts during the summer as a way of offering a gift to the community. There is no cost to attend (and no cost to the church) and people enjoy taking a short break for lunch while listening to relaxing music.

IDEA: Designate a Sunday at your church as Friendship Sunday.

Members want to share their faith and church family with their friends. Here is one way you can help them do it. One church held a Friendship Sunday that was promoted in the newsletter, from the pulpit, and in the bulletin for about four weeks prior to the day. Members were asked to each bring a friend, perhaps one without a church home. The entire service focused on friendships and included special music by a group of friends along with a Good News message that all friends could share. The service on Friendship Sunday filled the sanctuary and resulted in increased attendance the following weeks. How can you make it easy for members to invite friends to church?

IDEA: Pool your people and resources for a visitation blitz.

How did one church visit more than a hundred prospective families in an hour? They gathered names and addresses of visitors who had been to their church in the last few months. They grouped these addresses according to location, set a date for the "visitation blitz," and sent out volunteers from the church in teams of one and two to pass out literature and answer possible questions. Each team took five addresses and kept the visits intentionally short, between five and ten minutes each. The new prospects appreciated the personal touch. The volunteers enjoyed the evangelistic experience because it was a short-term commitment (about ninety minutes total, including instructions), it was nonthreatening, and it was a concrete way to share their faith.

IDEA: Advertise and evangelize by cleaning up the environment.

How do several churches advertise and evangelize in their community while providing an example of stewardship at the same time? By cleaning up one to two miles of local highway several times a year! By contacting your state highway department, you can find out what portion of a local highway near your church or town needs to be cleaned of litter. Members of your church pick up the area a couple of times a year, and the state puts up an Adopt-A-Highway sign with your church's name on it. If a desired section of highway is currently being cleaned by another group, you may want to place your name on a waiting list until the requested area is available.

IDEA: Create a pledge card to invite others to church.

It's sometimes easier to talk about evangelism than to put it into practice, but here is one idea for encouraging members to follow through on their good intentions of inviting others to church. Create an Invitation Pledge Card so that members can pledge to invite a certain number of people a year to church. It could include space to list prospect names and to set a goal. You might also want to provide a list of ideas and suggestions on *how* to invite others. Some churches offer support groups to affirm successes and offer encouragement for evangelism. How can you make it easy and encourage members to invite friends to your church?

IDEA: Do regular mailings to new residents in your community.

How do you get the names and addresses of all the new residents in town each month? One church gets a complete list from the local utility company of all homes that have just been connected to the town's water supply. They send each new resident a brochure about the church and put them on the church newsletter mailing list for six months. You also might want to check with your local electric company, city hall, post office, or Chamber of Commerce to see if they have lists available.

IDEA: Make it clear to visitors that they are welcome at most nonworship events.

Sometimes we assume that visitors and guests know that they are welcome at church functions, but that message is not always communicated. The words "you don't need to be a church member to attend" can let people know clearly that they are welcome. This applies to attending Bible studies, enrolling their children in Sunday school, serving on committees, and attending social events. Some churches treat visitors and regular guests virtually as members, giving them access to everything except voting rights and elected positions. Is your church open to nonmembers?

IDEA: Get new members off to a good start with a VIP treatment.

One way to decrease the anxiety level of newcomers to Sunday school or Sunday worship is to have others welcome them with special care and attention. One church uses a Newcomers Committee to greet visitors at the door, register them for classes, escort them to their new classroom, and introduce them to other students or members. Another church assigns a member to act as a friend to a new member, introducing the new person to others and showing him or her around the facility. This allows new members and guests to meet others in a nonthreatening environment while it tells them how unique and important they are to the church.

IDEA: Provide support to church members in nursing homes.

It is easy to forget about church members you don't see on a regular basis, especially those members in nursing homes. One way to bring these members to the attention of the congregation is to frequently publish a list of names and addresses of nursing home residents. This can encourage members to send them a card or letter and visit them on a regular basis. This concept also applies to members who are away or in the military, and would enjoy receiving mail from church friends. A Sunday school class could also "adopt" nursing home residents for a year.

EVENTS

IDEA: Hold large congregational meetings with members seated around tables.

Here's a way to increase membership involvement and satisfaction at your next annual meeting. Have your gathering in a large meeting room with the participants seated around tables. Designate a leader for each group of seven or eight people per table. Have the people at the table discuss and write down the strengths of the church, the weaknesses of the church, and positive ideas on how changes can be implemented. Later the leader gives a brief report to the group about what was discussed. Those at the meeting receive the satisfaction that comes from participation, and the church receives needed direction for the new year direct from the members. Participants feel that they are listened to, gain insights in the operation of the church, and get to know other members better. A more productive meeting is held, church business is conducted, and the meeting is more enjoyable for all concerned.

IDEA: Use ten words to help you plan your next event.

The next time you are planning an event, use ten words to guide your thinking. Let's say your committee is planning the annual Christmas dinner. Ask each committee member at the start of your meeting to write down ten words that describe the event. Then compare lists. Use the words to focus on what's most important in terms of the purpose of the event and on what you want people to get out of it. This technique gets your committee thinking about goals—the first step in planning any successful event.

IDEA: Open your event with bursting balloons.

On Rally Sunday, or during almost any festive church event, balloons can be utilized to open your gathering with a bang. Give each person a balloon and open the festivities with everyone popping their balloons at the same time.

THE CHURCH IDEA BOOK

IDEA: Give a price break for families.

One church offers families a special low price on admission to church events like dinners or concerts. An example: Any family unit will be admitted for $5, whether your family includes two or twelve people. Sometimes special Family Nights are offered. This practice encourages and rewards family togetherness and also increases total attendance at church events. Give families a price break at your next church event!

IDEA: Have participants present diplomas to each other following church seminars.

At the close of your next retreat or seminar, create some simple Certificates of Participation or Appreciation so that each person has a diploma for attending. Give the certificates out at random so that everyone has someone else's certificate. Then tell your people that they have the privilege of presenting a certificate with a traditional hug. It's a great way to end a Christian gathering with lots of love and warmth.

IDEA: Offer a weekly meal for singles of all ages.

If your church is like most, chances are there are many single people who eat alone and cook just for themselves every day. One idea to promote fellowship, Christian community, and to "feed the hungry" is to set aside one night a week when singles of all ages can come to church and share a meal. It could be just potluck or a planned menu. You might want to tie it in with choir practices or confirmation so that others benefit and don't have to rush to prepare a meal before going to church. For singles, sharing a meal together on a regular basis could be a real ministry!

IDEA: Give people an option with a Tuesday night Sunday school.

Because of limited space and the hectic schedules of working parents, one church offers Sunday school on Tuesday nights.

This offers single parents (or parents that work on Sunday) an opportunity for educating their children who might otherwise be forced to miss the experience. It also appeals to the volunteers who teach. They do not have to sacrifice family worship or personal Bible study opportunities offered only on Sunday.

IDEA: Inform people of the work of committees with a Church Council Expo.

Many people hesitate to join decision-making groups or committees in the church simply because they don't know the expectations, commitments, or job descriptions of the various positions. One church dealt with this situation by having a Church Council Expo, a day when each of the committees on the council (e.g., Stewardship, Youth, Property, Missions, and so on) sets up a booth in the church dining hall. After worship services, people are invited to browse the area, picking up brochures and talking to committee members at each booth. It can be an exciting, creative, and convenient way for people in church to meet committee members and get an idea of the broad ministry being carried on by the church.

IDEA: Add some "twists" to summer continuing education classes.

Offering summer continuing education classes is nothing new, but here are some new twists to the idea that you may want to consider. For example, one church offers summer classes for children and teens along with classes for adults. The classes run on Wednesday nights for one month. Another idea is to expand continuing education classes to a quarterly basis. Spring, fall, and winter months are also excellent times for people to be renewed and refreshed. And finally, how about targeting these classes to nonmembers, people who do not attend your church? This can be a nonthreatening way for them to set foot inside your church. Members can recruit their friends. Flyers can be sent to neighborhood homes.

IDEA: For Halloween, have teens go on a neighborhood scavenger hunt for food items.

One church combines fellowship, fun, and work for a good cause for teenage members each Halloween. The church writes up a specific list of food items and on Halloween sets teens loose in the neighborhood. The teens go in groups and compete to gather all food items on the list. The food collected is brought back to the church and is given to the local food shelf. The searchers spend the rest of the evening at the church enjoying pizza and movies.

IDEA: Offer free Friday night babysitting once a month as a community service.

If you are looking for ways to offer an appreciated service to members of your community, consider the act of babysitting. One church offers neighborhood parents a free evening of babysitting at the church as a community service. It offers different activities for different age groups from 6:00 P.M. to 10:00 P.M. It gives parents a breather and allows them to save the price of a sitter. It is one way to get new people acquainted with your church. Write down some rules and guidelines and give it a try!

FAMILY

IDEA: Use a "celebration marker" to mark church family events.

Celebration markers can help us observe important church events through visible signs as well as keep our eyes on goals we have set for our family of believers. Some ideas: Why not plant a maple tree every time membership increases 10 percent? Or add an evergreen for each new church addition? Or add a rose bush for each couple celebrating their 50th wedding anniversary? Or add a church decal on the bus for every one thousand miles it has survived? You can even have a special celebration service if you would like. Such "markers" remind us of God's continued presence and help us celebrate our victories of faith.

IDEA: Once a year have Family Month at your church.

One church honored and highlighted the importance of families by having a Family Month. During Sunday services, music was performed by families, coffee was served by families, and there was even a display of family photos for people to view. Other ideas could include a sermon/message by a husband and wife, some educational presentations by families, and a focus on family literature in the church library. Emphasis could also include how senior citizens or groups in your church are part of a family—so that members become aware that families take many forms.

IDEA: Use one night of the week as Family Night at church.

Sunday is the most active day for church activities, but for many churches Wednesday is running a very close second, with a full evening of activities. One church has made a special effort to turn Wednesday evening into church and family night. They serve a meal from 5:30 to 6:30 P.M. for fellowship and to help families in which one or both parents work outside the home. An Education Hour follows from 6:30 to 7:30 P.M. It includes a Bible study, confirmation, choir rehearsal and special educational programming. Starting at 7:30 P.M., there are activities and meetings. During this time committees get together, more choirs practice, and there are special activities for youth and young adults. Are Wednesdays at your church used to their full potential with something for all ages and interests?

IDEA: Offer a family retreat weekend.

How do you use the weekends to your advantage in promoting both the church and family togetherness? One congregation uses the facilities of a nearby church camp twice a year to hold weekend family retreats. Families relax together using indoor and outdoor sporting facilities. Meals are served as a group. Mini-worship events, such as movies and discussions on pertinent issues, offer time for nurture, support, and faith building.

FINANCIAL

IDEA: Ask members to bring a coffee mug to church.

Here's an innovative idea on how to be economical and ecological in the use of cups for coffee breaks. One church promoted "Bring Your Mug" Sunday and asked members to donate a coffee mug to be shared with the entire congregation for coffee breaks. The mugs were substituted for plastic foam or paper cups, which are not good for the environment. In requesting the donations, the church noted that because of the church's commercial dishwasher, members were NOT asked to donate stoneware, clay, or plastic mugs. Members were also reminded that because of the large number that would be donated and used, members could not plan on using the specific mug they donated. The church now has a growing collection of china mugs and no longer has the expense of buying cups on a regular basis.

IDEA: Challenge members to tithe following the example of the leaders in your congregation.

One church met the challenge to tithe by beginning with their leadership. The pastors, after pledging to tithe, challenged the Church Council to do the same. After announcing the commitments of the leadership, the congregation was then challenged to tithe for one month. Since the challenge, the percentage of giving over the next three months increased by 21 percent, 79 percent, and 38 percent respectively; an average increase of 43 percent per month!

IDEA: Take a special collection each Sunday for the needy.

Would you like your church to have the ability to financially help individuals and organizations in times of emergencies? One church met this challenge by establishing a Do Unto Others Fund. Each Sunday at the beginning of the service they take a special collection for their "DUO Fund." Before taking the collection, it is explained that it is not the regular collection, but a way of offering financial help to those in need. Worshipers are asked to drop in spare change or a dollar bill into coffee cans as they are passed around. (The coffee cans are used so that people know it is not the regular offering and because the sound of coins being dropped in the cans can be heard as encouragement to give.) The fund has enabled the church to help people pay rent, utility, medical bills, and so on. Church members are happy to contribute because they know that the money goes to a good cause without any administrative overhead. They also know that if they are ever in need, the church can help them financially as well as spiritually. The church collects and distributes over $10,000 a year in this manner.

IDEA: Ask your printer to help your church save money.

When you take church materials to a printing company, knowledge and cooperation with the printer can result in big savings. For example, untextured paper is cheaper than textured paper. And white paper is virtually always less expensive than colored stock. Recycled paper is even cheaper. Also look for ways to eliminate extra sheets by reducing the size of a page and including it on another sheet. And remember that it pays to shop around. Some printers are willing to give a 10 percent discount if you will give them the same work on a regular basis. One church cut the cost of a monthly newsletter from $210 to $125 by applying some of these ideas. Ask your printer for more ideas to stretch your printing budget!

IDEA: Give members the opportunity for automatic stewardship.

Have you ever wondered how to keep contributions coming in on a consistent basis, even though attendance is inconsistent? One possibility could be offering voluntary payroll deductions or automatic withdrawals for your members. Though some may object to this impersonal means of receiving contributions, others may see it as a responsible method for carrying out stewardship.

IDEA: Help pay for the cost of your monthly newsletter by allowing members to place small classified advertisements.

One way to generate income, provide a valuable service to members, and increase the value of your newsletter is to allow members to place nonbusiness classified ads in your church publication. One church provides this service to defray publication costs. They limit the size of the ad to twenty-five words, restrict it to noncommercial notices, and charge $5 per ad. Members use the ads to buy, sell, and trade household items, to rent rooms, and even to obtain babysitters from within the congregation. (The forty ads per issue generate $200 and pay for much of the printing expenses.)

IDEA: Let members help pay debts by "adopting a bill."

When money is short at the end or beginning of the year, one church has a practice of posting some financial needs on their bulletin board and inviting members to adopt and pay a bill. A lock box is provided near the list for donations. Members can choose between an ongoing bill or a one-time expense. By doing this, the church receives funds to pay creditors while giving members the opportunity to do something out of the ordinary to say thank-you to the church—or just to help out.

IDEA: Create a Wish List of SMALL things you need.

Members of your church will be happy to donate small items for use in the operation of the church. That's why one church created and posted a wish list of items that members could donate so that expenditures would be reduced. The list included toilet paper, light bulbs, cleaning supplies, coffee, file folders, and so on. Within a week, members generously responded and the church did not have to buy these items. They were able to put available funds toward meeting other needs. If your church is deep in the red, this is one way to get the red out.

IDEA: Designate a Sunday in September as "Catch-Up Sunday"—a time for members to bring pledges up-to-date.

If your church gets further and further behind financially as the year goes on, this year don't wait until December for people to make their financial pledges current. Using a postcard mailing and notices in bulletins and newsletters, create an expected time of financial renewal to remind people of their commitments. Members will also appreciate a nudge in September rather than all at once in December. One secret of Catch-Up Sunday is that it gets noticed and is a total church effort.

IDEA: Use designated envelopes to increase giving.

It was customary for one church to collect monies for World Hunger and the local food shelf by having ushers take a free will offering as people exited the church service. Bills or excess change were tossed in a basket, assuming people remembered or had funds available. When special envelopes (prominently printed with the given cause) were handed out before the church service, giving increased dramatically. In one year, monies for the local food shelf doubled; monies for World Hunger tripled.

IDEA: Get paid for reviewing church curriculum.

Though many pastors complain about church curriculum, few realize the impact they can have on material before it is published. Church affiliated publishing houses still have reviewers check manuscripts for content, theology, age appropriateness, and inclusivity. If you would like to see what's being published and enjoy learning in the process, contact your local religious publishing house for information. Honorariums and qualifications for reviewers may vary.

FUND RAISING

IDEA: Appeal to the five senses to raise money.

If you were going to give money for a worthy cause, would you rather give it for an object you could taste, feel, and see—or would you prefer giving it to an idea? One church proved to itself which method worked better. When they simply asked for contributions to buy a piano, they raised less than $100 in a year's time. However, when they put up a picture of a piano keyboard and sold each key for $35, they had 75 percent of the funds in a few months.

IDEA: Offer the public a chance to sell at your next rummage sale.

One church found a way to increase both revenue and public participation at their annual rummage sale. The church placed an ad in the local newspaper offering the public the opportunity to rent a table at the rummage sale for just $10. The idea not only helped increase attendance by making the event larger, but it was also a great mixer for members and nonmembers.

IDEA: Hold your next fund raiser outdoors during the tourist season.

Several churches make it a point to have their annual church auction or bazaar during the height of the tourist season. Church members donate handcrafted quilts, garden produce, homemade pies, baked goods, antiques, toys, and even used cars. They advertise well in advance and sell food and refreshments on the day of the sale. And instead of keeping things indoors, they move them outside under the protection of a large tent to make the event more visible. Selling wares to tourists has doubled and tripled their profits. Is there a community celebration in your city that you could use to generate attendance?

IDEA: Use $50 as an always available loan to help individuals do their own fund raisers.

Here's a way of making a fifty-dollar bill live forever so that it can be used to earn extra income for the church year after year. This started at one church when a member donated $50 to the church and designated it as "seed money" for individual fund raising projects. When members desire, they borrow the $50 and use it as an investment for the materials they need for their project. The money can be used anytime by an individual or a group of people, just doing their own thing on their own. It gets used repeatedly by individuals over the course of a year and then it is returned so that others can use it also. From time to time the church newsletter lists how the money was used and the results achieved, and encourages others to put their time and talents to work for the church.

IDEA: Let members offer their time and talents to others through a silent auction.

One church used the talents of their members, increased fellowship, and raised $1,500 for building improvements all at the same time. Here is how it worked: (1) Members wrote down on a piece of paper an item, talent, or service that could be sold to others in the congregation. They included such things as a progressive dinner for eight, a week at a lake home (meals included), and yard work services. (2) This information was posted on a large bulletin board in fellowship hall. (3) Members wrote silent bids of the item or talent they wished to purchase (including the dollar amount) and placed the bids in a box. (4) On the designated date, the stewardship committee opened up the sealed bids and awarded each item or service to the highest bidder. (5) The "winners" were listed in the bulletin with the item they received. No dollar amounts were listed.

IDEA: Launch an "Eliminate the Negative" campaign to wipe out your financial deficit.

One church was about $8,000 in the red at the end of the year. To remedy this, they launched an "Eliminate the Negative" campaign that asked members to contribute what they could to make up for the shortfall. This was communicated through letters, postcards, newsletter articles, bulletin inserts, and was mentioned from the pulpit. Progress was announced each week. Once members knew of the challenge, they pitched in and within a month the deficit was eliminated. Regular contributions also increased during the following months, and one year later the church had 105 percent of its budget from member contributions.

IDEA: Utilize the power of prayer and people with a Miracle Sunday.

One church was heading for financial trouble and scheduled a Miracle Sunday, when they prayed that members would donate $10,000 above the regular Sunday offering. Miracle Sunday was promoted for about one month in advance as members were educated about weekly expenses and the needs of the ministry. Members were also given Promise Notes that they could use if they had the desire to give, but didn't have the funds at the time. When Miracle Sunday arrived, the church received over $12,000 in cash and more in pledges.

IDEA: Pass the collection plate and ask members to take a five-dollar bill out and multiply it for the church.

In order to generate funds for a special cause, some churches fill a collection plate with new five-dollar bills and pass the plate among members encouraging them to remove a bill. Participants are asked to use the money to finance their own personal fund raising effort. Members use their ideas, talents, and time to multiply the $5 and return it—plus what they have made on it for the church. One Catholic church turned $2,000 into $5,000 in this manner.

IDEA: Ask members to invest a dollar of their own money in a fund raising project for the church.

A Lutheran church in Pennsylvania generated $1,500 by asking their members to take $1 of their own money and multiply it any way they desired for the church. A poster listed services so that members could network and communicate their talents and offerings.

IDEA: Let members taste food to raise money.

Several Minnesota churches have raised $750 to $900 in one night by having their members taste food. In the one-hour session the volunteers taste and rank food products varying from cold cereal to cake, always with the option to pass or stop eating. (Usually two or three bites is adequate.) The company sponsoring the taste test supplies food, setup, and most cleanup. The church provides the kitchen and from 25 to 105 tasters. Check your local Yellow Pages for a company in your area that could use some volunteers.

IDEA: Sponsor an Annual Dinner at $50 per plate.

One church has been sponsoring an annual fund raiser for their church building fund for the past four years. The dinner is catered at a nearby facility. Entertainment includes a piano player and singer during hors d'oeuvres, a comic or singer or band after dinner, and a guest singing appearance by the pastors of the church. The dinner raises between $4,000 and $5,000 per year. The proceeds go toward reducing the principal of the building mortgage.

MEMBERSHIP

IDEA: Have members bring their garden produce to church.

One church uses a produce table to keep the congregation focused on world hunger. During the summer, extra produce from home gardens is sold at the table on Sunday morning. Proceeds from the sales benefit a world hunger appeal or local food shelves. Seasonal fare, such as pumpkins or holly, can be brought in year-round as a continued reminder of God's blessings to us and our mission to others.

IDEA: Have a Bible verse focus for your church for an entire year.

Have you ever considered finding a special verse in the Bible that could act as a theme for activities throughout the coming year? One church did just that and printed it in every bulletin and newsletter. Several programs were built around it as well as some sermons.

IDEA: Help members become more aware of utilizing memorials.

Are your members familiar with various memorials offered at your church? Do they know what memorials are? An easy way to answer both questions is to provide a pamphlet that explains the reasons for memorials and the different memorials available through the church. You could add a one- or two-line description of each, helping the family make a choice according to the interests of the deceased. You could also provide Recognition Gifts that would be given in honor of special occasions such as anniversaries, weddings, birthdays, and baptisms. When a memorial or recognition gift is given, a card can be sent to the giver, thereby acknowledging the gift.

IDEA: Create a video for use in your annual stewardship drive.

As part of a stewardship drive, one church wanted to show members where their contributions go and the many activities that take place at church during the week. They accomplished this by asking members to bring cameras to church and to take photos of activities for several weeks. The church furnished slide film and had it developed. Instead of creating a slide show, however, they chose to produce a fifteen-minute video. Using the slides as a starting point, a script was written and then the services of the local community cable system were utilized to turn the slides into a video production, all at a cost of next to nothing. The production gave members a chance to work together and also learn about making a video. Many cities have cable community television stations that give free or low-cost access to nonprofit organizations. (And they are really glad to help!) You might even be able to have your church video broadcast to your community on local cable. Give this idea to the person at your church with an interest in video production!

IDEA: Decrease inactivity by noticing who is absent.

People like to be noticed when they are absent. Think of it this way: after being gone from church for weeks and having nobody contact you, how would you feel? Would you be eager to return to the church? The church is a family and family members need to know that they belong, are loved, and are missed when they are not there. Sometimes all it takes is a phone call from a thoughtful member, or a quick note on a postcard from a pastor or staff person. Do they need a ride? Is there an illness? Brainstorm some simple ways you can say: We miss you!

IDEA: Kick off fall activities with a church picnic or carnival.

One congregation welcomes members back from the summer slump with a picnic and carnival offered the second Sunday in September. Sunday school students receive free meal tickets for a picnic lunch. Clowns, music groups, a youth lip sync, a water balloon toss, a cakewalk, and a softball game provide some of the entertainment. Church council committees divide up tasks and work assignments. The monetary goal is simple: break even.

IDEA: Encourage members to take the lead in meeting needs using church resources.

God cares for people through people. Challenge your members to use your church and its resources in meeting the needs of others. Invite them to combine efforts with other members to help the homeless, visit the sick, or raise money for the poor. If they feel that they are called to a ministry, let them know that they are welcome to begin a group or task force within the church. You can provide meeting space, people, ideas, and support in empowering your membership to reach out!

PROPERTY

IDEA: Expand your church by going underground.

When one church was interested in expanding their facility, they discovered it is less expensive to expand a basement area underground rather than build an addition above ground. There are no windows or roof on a basement addition, so this keeps the costs down—and upkeep is certainly much less. It is worth investigating if you are planning to expand.

IDEA: Provide designated parking for church guests.

Most churches have limited vehicle parking space for members on Sunday mornings, so where do guests and first-time visitors get to park? One solution some churches have tried is to have reserved parking spots for first-time visitors. It is a quiet way of welcoming guests and showing that they are important, while keeping them out of the battle for limited parking spaces.

IDEA: Make specific requests for large needs within your church.

If you need something for your church office or building, why not ask? A church wanted to purchase a computer system, but because of limited funds, the acquisition was postponed for months. Finally, in desperation, they asked if someone would like to make a donation for the cause. They were rewarded with a beautiful, state-of-the-art piece of equipment from a member, saving $1,500 from their budget. Another church wanted a camera for use with youth events. They put the request in the Sunday bulletin. Within three weeks they had two 35mm cameras and a VCR recorder! The gifts, though used, were in excellent shape. One note: the more specific your request, the better. You may get even more than you bargained for.

40

IDEA: Use parking lot attendants on Sunday mornings.

To keep parking hassles down to a minimum and church traffic safe and efficient, why not use parking lot attendants to direct the way? Attendants provide assistance not only outside in the lot, but can also answer questions about Sunday school, adult forums, or other activities taking place inside the church. Attendants can wear patches or some other visible identification. Not only does this keep things moving on busy or unusual Sundays, but it's also a good chance to offer a friendly welcome to visitors and members.

IDEA: Make your church visitor-friendly by creating directional signs and maps throughout the building.

Whether your church building is small or large, signs directing visitors are always welcome. As an experiment, go to a church you have never visited during the week and try to find the church office—or an open door that will get you in the building—it can be frustrating! Ask someone unfamiliar with your church to help you in placing signs and for suggestions on how to make your building more friendly to first-timers.

PUBLICITY

IDEA: Ask a newspaper to do a story about your church.

Instead of advertising in your local newspaper, why not get cheaper and better coverage for church events by having the newspaper cover the event for you? One pastor talked to an editor about advertising a stress seminar. Instead of advertising, however, the editor suggested doing a front-page story about the event. Another church gained newspaper publicity through an article about their Sunday school program. Think of an upcoming event or something unique about your church and communicate the idea to your local newspaper.

IDEA: Promote an event by giving out free tickets.

Here's an idea on how you can get all your members involved in generating publicity for your next church event. Instead of printing posters or flyers, print free tickets that are given away by members to friends, relatives, and coworkers. Tickets work great because they give the time, date, and place in writing so that people can't say they forgot. They are more likely to be held onto and used. Few people throw away tickets that are given to them. They are also smaller than posters and easy for members to carry around and distribute—a nonthreatening way to invite others to a church event!

IDEA: Videotape events to promote the same events in the future.

One way to promote youth events is by showing videotapes of the same event from past years. For example, to promote an upcoming ski trip, one church showed videos taken from the last ski trip. On Sunday morning, they put a television set in a prominent traffic area so that both parents and youth could enjoy the rerun. This makes participants "instant stars" and shows others how much fun the event can be, in living color and at a small cost.

IDEA: Sponsor a program or event in exchange for publicity.

How can you promote your church and support a gospel music ministry for less than the cost of a guest soloist? One way is to buy a "spot" on your local religious radio station to advertise during a program that captures the values and interests of your church. Commercial spots on small radio stations can be purchased for as little as ten dollars.

IDEA: Give out grocery bags to promote your food drive.

Most churches have food drives during the year when they ask members to bring cans or boxes of food for the needy. But sometimes well-intentioned church members forget. To solve this problem, one church used a unique method to promote their food drive. They created an eight-by-ten-inch flyer about the food drive and then stapled the flyer to a regular brown grocery bag. The bags were given out to church members after Sunday services. Members were asked to place the bag in their kitchen or leave it in their car to serve as a reminder. Many of the bags were filled with groceries and made it back to the church.

IDEA: Use ready-to-mail postcards for members to promote events.

If you want to make it easy for members to invite guests to special church events, try creating a ready-to-mail postcard that serves as an invitation and flyer all in one. The format gives members room to sign their name and even write a short note. It also contains the time, date, and place of the event with important details. Members pick up cards in the church office a week or two before the event, add a stamp, and mail some to friends.

IDEA: Ask store owners to put a flyer promoting your next church event inside bags containing customer purchases.

Here's a brown bag promotion that gets results every time! With the help of store owners or managers who belong to your church you can obtain free publicity for your next church event. Prepare promotional flyers and ask those who operate stores to display the flyers at the check-out counter, post them in windows, or better yet, put them in bags containing customer purchases.

IDEA: Direct visitors to your church with small signs along the road.

On a vacation recently, my wife and I were looking for a place to worship. As we drove down the street, we saw several small signs with the name of a church, worship times, and directions. We decided to follow-up the next morning, even though it wasn't our denomination. The church was small, but literally overflowing with out-of-town visitors. Obviously, their one-person marketing staff knew something about leading people.

IDEA: Save money by using postcards instead of letters.

If you are sending out a short letter or reminder to members of your church, it could pay to use postcards instead. First-class postage alone is 40 percent less, besides the additional savings in envelopes and stationery. Continuous, perforated postcards can easily be set up on a computer with mail-merge software. Or, divide an 8-by-11-inch sheet of paper into fourths and type your message in each of the four boxes. Run it through your copier with card stock, cut into postcards and mail.

IDEA: Print information about your church on business cards.

If you want members of your congregation to invite others to your church, here is how you can make it easy for them. Have some business cards printed containing the name of your church, address, worship times, phone number, what makes your church unique, and any other information you feel is important. The small cards are much easier for members to carry around than brochures. They fit easily into a wallet or purse. And they can be given out easily during the course of a casual conversation. Don't forget that each card has two sides—use the reverse for an additional message. These inexpensive cards can also be used to promote church events. Get some into the hands of your members with suggestions on how to use them.

IDEA: Make flyers available for everyone to distribute.

Your entire congregation can participate in promoting your next big event at church. Create enough three-by-five-inch promotional flyers for everybody to have about ten each. Ask your people to take ten, leave them in their cars, and place them around town. Ideas for distribution: leave flyers on tables at fast-food places, in waiting rooms, at libraries, on bulletin boards, on telephone poles, as an insert when paying bills, anywhere there is a counter or table. They can also give the flyers to friends.

IDEA: Get a special easy-to-remember phone number for your church.

One affordable way to make your church phone number memorable and meaningful at the same time is to request a number from the phone company that spells out a message. For example, you could list the church name, if it was "Trinity" (874-6489) or "Central" (236-8725) or another seven-letter word not in use. You could also use it as a hotline number or to highlight a special congregational emphasis, such as "mission" (647-7466) or "prayers" (772-9377). Easy-to-remember numbers are also available (e.g., 333-1000), which allow you to remember the number without picking up the phone book.

IDEA: Join together with other local churches for joint publicity.

There are several inexpensive, yet effective ways to make your church service times visible to others in the community. One way is to have the churches in your area put together a brochure listing church names, addresses, denominations, and service times. These can be distributed through your local Welcome Wagon or the Chamber of Commerce to people moving into your community. For additional local exposure, be sure your church is listed in the Yellow Pages.

IDEA: Utilize your local cable television station to promote your church.

How would you like to broadcast your own video program on your local cable network free of charge? Many cable companies are required to offer a certain amount of air time for Community Access Programming as one of their services. This allows people of your community a chance to voice opinions, concerns, appreciation, or creative ideas on cable at no charge. You can even use the cable company's facilities and taping equipment after completing a short training course. While there is a charge for the certification courses, use of the equipment is free thereafter.

SEASONS

IDEA: Give out a reminder at midweek Lenten services.

One church helped members get extra meaning from Lent by giving out a symbol of Lent after each midweek evening service. Volunteers from the church constructed over two hundred wooden crosses that were given out on Ash Wednesday. During the following midweek services, worshipers were given a symbol to take home and place beneath their cross. One week a rock was given, another week a nail, the next week a purple cloth—each item tied into the sermon and the Easter story.

IDEA: Create a giant holiday card for everyone to sign.

Each Christmas, one church creates a giant Christmas card, which sits on a table in the narthex for everyone to sign. It is then sent to the congregation's missionaries. It can be fun to create the card and people enjoy writing a personal message during the holiday season.

Another similar idea is to create a large card for a holiday such as Easter or Thanksgiving. Members sign the card and include their favorite childhood memory on it that relates to the holiday. The card is then presented to residents of a nursing home. It's a nice way to remember forgotten people on a holiday. (This idea also works for Mother's Day and Father's Day.) You might also tell the news media about your project.

IDEA: Help church members extend the season of Christmas.

Christmas often comes and goes before people have a chance to enjoy the entire season. One way to savor the season a little longer would be to extend the season in which we celebrate. There is even a historical example for our use. The Council of Tours in A.D. 567 established Christmas as a twelve-day season, beginning December 25 and running through January 5. (January 6 is the Festival of the Epiphany of Our Lord.) Daily family devotions would make each day significant, as would the use of candles. Presents could be rationed. There are materials for use before Christmas, as well, including Advent calendars, devotions, and family activities.

IDEA: Use an evergreen tree to tie together church seasons.

One church uses the evergreen tree to tie together the life and death and resurrection of Jesus. How do they do it? During Advent and Christmas the tree anticipates and welcomes Jesus' birth. During Epiphany the tree becomes an "Epiphany Pole"—all the branches are cut off and the tree remains standing solo and erect in the sanctuary, always before the congregation as Jesus' presence in the world. In Lent, the Epiphany Pole is cut into two pieces to form the cross where Jesus died. From life to death to life, the tree becomes an appropriate continuum of our life and faith.

IDEA: Use pretzels to teach about prayer.

What do pretzels have to do with prayer? Everything! Pretzels were supposedly invented during the Middle Ages by a monk who wanted to remind people how to pray. The twists were used to show people how their hands were to be folded during prayer. It's a tasty and lasting way to introduce the topic for a children's sermon or for a Lenten theme.

Another food item appropriate for the Easter season is rock candy, which can be used to remind children of the rock rolled away from the tomb on Easter morning.

IDEA: Supply church Christmas cards so that members can invite friends and relatives to Christmas services.

You can make it easy for church members to invite friends and family to Christmas Eve or Christmas Day services by supplying church Christmas cards that carry an invitation to attend church services. Cards can be created especially for this purpose, or can be purchased at a store and imprinted. Besides the regular Christmas greeting/message, the inside of the card can give the address of the church, service times, sermon title, and so on. Church members can pick up these cards in the church office and mail them to friends and family who may not have a church home.

IDEA: Invite people to share ideas on how to make the season of Christmas more meaningful.

It's often difficult for families and individuals to find Christmas traditions that are both meaningful and enjoyable. Why not use your entire congregation to help? Invite people to share ideas, or have a contest titled "The Best Christmas Tradition Ever." Each entrant completes this sentence on a three-by-five card. The ideas can be shared in the weekly bulletin or newsletter, included in the calendar, featured in the local newspaper, or collected and distributed in booklet form to the entire community.

IDEA: Encourage members to celebrate Thanksgiving all year with a "Thanksgiving Jar."

Here's a way to celebrate your thankfulness to God all year long and make it especially meaningful at Thanksgiving. Encourage each family or individual to create a decorated jar or container with a hole in the top. Whenever something good happens in a person's life, the person writes it down with his or her name and puts it into the container along with some coins. During the Thanksgiving meal, the slips of paper listing things people are thankful for are read. The coins in the container are given to a charity to help pay for a Thanksgiving meal for the needy.

IDEA: Have your committee, circle, or group celebrate Thanksgiving once a month.

As an opening exercise for a monthly meeting of a church group or committee, have members write down five things they are thankful for and have them share them with the rest of the group.

Do this once a month for a whole year. This helps people focus on the blessings of God on a monthly basis and lifts spirits prior to the start of a meeting.

IDEA: Utilize summer as a season of personal growth by using the talents and resources of your congregation.

Resources close to home are often those easiest to overlook. One church takes advantage of their local talent and knowledge by offering summer classes taught by lay people in the church. The classes are similar to community education classes, running from one to four weeks and ranging from financial planning, to Filipino cooking, to basic auto mechanics.

IDEA: Collect donations for the needy at Christmas by using a Mitten Tree.

Here is a unique way to decorate a tree and collect donations for the needy at the same time. All your church has to do is put up a Christmas tree and decorate it with donations of gloves, scarves, and mittens. Later, the mittens and other cold weather items are given to a charity for distribution to the homeless.

IDEA: Offer a holiday meal at your church for all those who don't have a place to go.

One Thanksgiving, a pastor announced from the pulpit that all church members and friends who did not have a place to go for Thanksgiving dinner could come to the church and a meal would be prepared there. One member of the congregation was in charge of all the arrangements. You could make a similar offer for a Christmas dinner. Sometimes we focus on the needy and homeless during the holiday seasons and overlook the fact that there are many congregational members without a place to go for the holidays.

IDEA: Merge your choir with the choir of another church for a special holiday concert.

The results are always impressive when church choirs join forces. You can put this into practice by inviting a nearby church to join yours for local Christmas caroling in a nursing home, school, or neighborhood. It is one thing that churches can do together and is appreciated by all recipients. Perhaps this could be a new Christmas tradition with one of your church neighbors. Get together and start planning! No one ever seems to get tired of hearing Christmas songs sung by a choir! This works well for a community-wide sunrise service, too.

IDEA: Consider additional performances of your annual Sunday school Christmas program in locations away from your church.

Most churches have an annual Christmas Program in which Sunday school children sing and perhaps act out a portion of the Christmas story. It is a lot of work for just one performance. How about considering two shows the same day so that more people can enjoy the Christmas story and all the effort that goes into telling it? You could bus the children to a nearby school, nursing home, or a senior citizens apartment building. Even hospitals have auditoriums that could be used. You could even advertise and open up a performance to the public.

IDEA: Survey holiday visitors at your church so you know what type of advertising works best.

Do you ever struggle with your holiday advertising budget, wondering where to spend those precious dollars? One way to get valuable feedback is to ask visitors who attend your Christmas services how they found out about your church and chose to attend. A brief survey in the bulletin works great for this. Get the facts in writing and next year you won't be wondering how to advertise.

IDEA: Use a lighted Christmas tree to remember special people.

One church lights up lives-by lighting up a Christmas tree with bulbs and lights in memory or honor of a friend or loved one. Lights are lit from December 1 through December 25, and the names of all individuals honored or remembered are offered in prayer during Christmas services. It is also used as a fund raiser ($10 per bulb) with the proceeds going toward food and clothing for the needy.

IDEA: Offer a "family night" at your church on New Year's Eve.

Members of your church might appreciate a refreshing alternative to traditional New Year's gatherings by spending the evening with church friends and family. It could be a game night, hymn sing, prayer-a-thon, worship service, or a combination of these activities.

SOCIAL

IDEA: Give people another person's name tag at the start of a gathering and have them find their own and meet that person.

The next time you want people to get to know others at a meeting, think about switching name tags. As your people enter the room, have them sign in at the registration table, but give each the name tag of another guest. Tell them before the meeting begins to find their own name tag and get to know the person wearing it. You can follow the exchange of name tags by having each person introduce his or her new friend to the group.

IDEA: Use blank church walls to hang paintings of member artists.

Have you ever thought of using those blank church walls in the narthex or meeting room for an art gallery? One church regularly features local artists who display their work at the church. Open houses are held and it is promoted in the church newsletter. The paintings are displayed for one month, giving time for members to enjoy the masterpieces while gaining recognition for the artists. It beautifies the church, promotes the arts, and allows people to enjoy the talents of fellow members in a social atmosphere.

IDEA: Have members get to know each other better by holding a Hobby Night.

If you are looking for a way to help church members become better acquainted with each other, scheduling a Hobby Night is one way to increase communication and comfort levels among members. Sharing hobbies provides a nonthreatening way for people to talk about themselves and their interests. The event could also be advertised to the public and could draw some new faces to your church.

IDEA: Encourage the exchange of names during morning greeting time.

If your church is one that takes a few minutes during Sunday services for members to greet one another, here is a simple idea on how you can encourage people to start "connecting" with each other. From the pulpit, be specific and ask members to say "hello" and exchange names. These instructions from the pastor are nonthreatening and "free" people to go beyond a one-word greeting and handshake.

IDEA: Challenge your members to "risk" a new introduction every Sunday for one month.

There is an individual at a church who makes it a point to introduce herself to a church visitor or unfamiliar member every Sunday. She makes four new friends every month. Perhaps you might want to challenge your members from the pulpit or through your newsletter to do the same. People are hungry for fellowship and this is one way each person can make a difference.

IDEA: As an opening group activity, have people introduce themselves with their name and a common item.

This name association exercise is a helpful way for learning and remembering names of others in a group. It begins with each person giving their first name, following it with an item you might find at an old general store that begins with the same first letter of the alphabet. For example, "My name is Hilda and I'm going to buy a huge Havana cigar." The next person gives their name and purchase, repeating the names and items given before them. By the time each person is introduced, almost anyone can repeat the entire list of names.

IDEA: Have group introductions include the meaning of a name and a favorite fairy tale.

Have members of a group give their entire name with the meaning and significance of first and middle names. (Who were you named after?) As a second part of this process, each person shares their favorite fairy tale, explaining which character they relate to and why.

IDEA: During introductions have people share their favorite P's.

Have each person share their favorite PLACE, favorite PERSON, and favorite PASTIME, recreation, or hobby. Since the first person sets the tone, choose someone who feels comfortable sharing with others. Encourage people to say as little or as much as they feel comfortable sharing with the group.

IDEA: Play "balloon volleyball" as a recreational event at church.

To play balloon volleyball, divide participants into two teams. A low sheet or net separates them. The players either sit on chairs or on the floor. A balloon is used as the volleyball and is hit back and forth over the net by the two teams. A point is scored when the balloon touches the ground. The first team to score ten points is the winner.

IDEA: Play "Drop It," a guessing game, as a social activity.

All you need to do is stand behind a sheet and drop objects on the floor while participants guess what was dropped. They write their guesses on a sheet of paper. Use about fifteen common items like a golf ball, a dime, a pencil, a piece of wood, a book, and a spoon. The person who correctly guesses the most items, wins.

IDEA: Try "Tissue Racing" as an indoor relay race.

Tissue racing is a relay race with tissue paper carried on tablespoons. The tissue paper is about two inches square and sits on a pillow at one end of the room. It gets carried on tablespoons across the room to a coffee cup, which sits on a table. The tissue must not be touched by anything. If it falls off, the tissue must be picked up by the spoon.

IDEA: Help people get acquainted by putting puzzle pieces together.

Before the gathering begins, cut up several large pictures (advertisements, postcards, photos) into several pieces and give each person a piece as they enter the room. Ask everyone to complete his or her puzzle before the function begins by locating individuals holding the other pieces. Each group of a puzzle could later become a committee or discussion group. It's a nice way to form groups and help people get better acquainted at the same time.

IDEA: When you need to break a large group into smaller segments, ask participants to find a common bond.

As your participants enter the room, ask them to locate and pair up with another person born the same month. Or ask those with the same color shoes to form a group.

IDEA: Have people get to know others by collecting autographs.

Give each person a pencil and paper as they enter the room. Ask them to get the autographs of all the people present before the session begins.

IDEA: Have people mix in a large group by searching for matching cards.

Using a deck of playing cards or even a set of Monopoly game property cards, give a card to each person entering the room and ask him or her to locate matching card holders.

IDEA: Break the ice by having people in a group locate the other half of a popular pair.

As people enter the room, give them a card with the name of half a common pair written on it. Examples: Adam and Eve, Jack and Jill, Salt and Pepper, and so on. Ask each person to match the pair before the meeting starts.

IDEA: As a get-acquainted activity, have people draw the face of one person in the group.

Give all participants a paper and pencil, and have them form a circle. Give them two minutes to draw the face or profile of the person on their right. Have them write the name of the person on the back of the paper and give you the drawing. Later, you mix up the papers and have people try to pick out their own portrait.

SPIRITUAL

IDEA: Encourage members to share their faith before the congregation.

During worship services, one church has pre-arranged with a different member each week to come forward and talk about his or her faith for five minutes. It is both refreshing and inspiring to hear someone talk of their faith; and the speaker as well as the audience benefits.

IDEA: Increase congregational biblical knowledge with a "Verse of the Month."

If you are looking for a way to increase the Bible knowledge of your members, have a "Verse of the Month" in your newsletter, bulletin, or even on a banner in your church to create awareness of God's Word. You could also focus on a book of the Bible every month. Along with this focus, create a few activities that people can use to grow in the Word. It is often easier to learn by breaking up the learning into twelve parts. And it's exciting to look back at the end of twelve months to see all that has been accomplished.

IDEA: Begin your day in prayer before distractions begin and encourage your members to do the same.

If you struggle to set aside time for prayer or Bible reading, it may help to start first thing in the morning several hours before work begins. Even though it may be difficult to get up before sunrise, there are several advantages to praying first thing in the morning. It is intentional, it sets a nice tone for the day, it is focused (no one is up to distract you and it is quiet), and it never gets lost in the shuffle of doing other things. If you absolutely need extra sleep, wake up for your devotional time and go back to bed later.

IDEA: Base some of your Sunday morning church prayers on the headlines in your local newspaper.

One effective way to pray for the needs of others in the world and in your community is by reading the daily newspaper. The stories, editorials, headlines, comics, and the sports section can be used as intercessory or personal prayer. Events in other nations can elicit a prayerful thanks or a prayer request that people in our own nation may be more responsible in making social decisions. Stories closer to home may evoke feelings of concern or sympathy, forgiveness or repentance. This idea is an excellent weekly project for a confirmation class.

IDEA: Let your people offer their own prayers along with the offering.

If you want to do something different to get your members involved in the prayers of the church, try this idea. Small pieces of paper are provided so that those who wish can write a prayer or a thanksgiving for a prayer answered, and include it with the offering. This simple idea says (1) that prayers and thanksgiving are ways to remember how God is working in our lives, (2) that concerns need to be "handed over" to God, and (3) that prayers come from the body of believers who live out their faith on a day-by-day basis. The prayers can be used with other prayers during the service or selected in advance. They can also be used in intercessory prayer during the week—individually or with other staff members.

IDEA: Light a candle on your altar and keep it burning each Sunday until a situation is resolved.

We need to have hope and remember that God is working in all situations. That is the reason to light a candle of hope or remembrance to let your congregation know that God will provide an answer for a specific issue. It could be until a recession ends, when a cure is found for a specific disease, until people who are away return to the congregation, or until an urgent congregational need is met. The candle, which can be dedicated in a brief ceremony, can also serve as silent testimony to your congregation's faith in God while saying that prayer does make a difference.

IDEA: Let the Spirit of God guide business decisions.

While many look to the Holy Spirit for guidance in making individual decisions, why not gather as a group to seek the Spirit's guidance in making corporate decisions? Begin by presenting available facts at a gathering, which in itself is viewed as more of a worship service than a meeting. The Spirit may move people to agree or disagree with an action based on the facts, but the important thing is that each person listens to the voice of God. Corporate guidance can also be used to aid individuals with personal decisions; a staff person may choose to seek another vocation or a couple may wonder if they are ready for marriage. All are opportunities to gather as a group to hear the voice of God and let the Spirit guide our actions.

TIME MANAGEMENT

IDEA: Gain time by reducing interruptions.

Leading experts estimate that each interruption can take away twenty minutes from a given task (to resume with the same concentration you had before the interruption). To avoid such delays: (1) block out an hour every day where you do not receive phone calls (unless an emergency), (2) if you do not have a secretary, turn on the answering machine, schedule a time to return phone calls, perhaps from 2:00 P.M. to 3:00 P.M. daily, (3) let other office staff know your "un-interruptible hour," and (4) come in an hour earlier or stay later than set office hours.

IDEA: Use minutes to keep informed rather than attending meetings.

Keeping minutes of meetings not only tracks the business transpiring, but can also keep others updated in a timely manner. After committees have recorded their minutes, distribute them to others affected by the committee's work. Doing so (1) keeps others informed, (2) saves reporting time at meetings—people can simply ask questions if they need something clarified, (3) helps committees coordinate efforts for ministry, (4) highlights the ministry taking place, and (5) provides idea starters for others.

IDEA: Offer monthly meetings instead of services-on-demand.

Instead of offering instruction on baptism, communion, and premarital counseling on an individual basis to parishioners, offer the same classes on a monthly basis. For example, offer a baptism preparation class the second Sunday of each month. People unable to attend simply wait a month for the next meeting. This saves hours a month for the pastor, frees up nights, and allows for flexibility in special cases. It also gives people options and responsibility for attending.

IDEA: Offer a regular drop-in time for members to come to the church and spend some time talking to the pastor.

It is sometimes difficult for a church member to get an opportunity to talk to his or her pastor. Sundays are very busy and during the rest of the week a pastor's time is heavily scheduled. One church decided to open up some "talking time" for the pastor and members by reserving Tuesday afternoons (3:00 P.M. to 6:00 P.M.) as a drop-in time to chat with the pastor. It is handled on a first-come, first-served basis and visits are twenty minutes. Members come to the church to share their ideas, concerns, and questions with the pastor. In the process, both the pastor and member get to know each other a bit better. And members know that the time is always there to talk, with no appointment necessary.

IDEA: Rid yourself of junk mail by banning it from church.

A quick way to deal with excess mail is to keep it from getting to the office in the first place. Get rid of "junk" mail by filling out a form at the post office that will remove you from third-class mailing lists. You can also contact the Direct Marketing Association, P.O. Box 3861, Grand Central Station, New York, NY 10163, to keep your name off the data base mailing lists that are sold from company to company.

IDEA: Free yourself from being conscious about time by purchasing an alarm watch.

Have you ever found yourself distracted by watching the clock, waiting for your next meeting or appointment to begin? If your time consciousness gets in the way of your work, why not buy an inexpensive alarm watch? Set the alarm or stop watch for the designated time and work undistracted until it's time to leave. The watch can also be used as a guideline for prayer time, reading time, study time, or meetings. It's an easy way to keep your eyes where they should be—on your work.

VOLUNTEERS

IDEA: Create a Volunteer Room for workers to help out.

One church holds down costs by utilizing a Volunteer Room where members can come anytime to help staff on current projects. It is equipped with desks, phones, files, and work areas along with lists of work to be done and instructions on how to do it. This gives members the freedom to give of their time and talent to accomplish necessary projects on a drop-in basis (as most churches always have extra work for volunteers). Minimum supervision is needed and the extra room area provides space to get work done without getting in the way.

IDEA: If you need some volunteers, ask for them.

It is amazing what happens sometimes when you ask for help. One church needed some volunteers to help straighten up the sanctuary after Sunday services. They printed a request in the Sunday bulletin for volunteers to come in on Mondays and replace hymnals in the racks and clean up around the church. As a result of the notice, the church secretary was flooded with offers of help. The church gained enough Monday volunteers for several months and the custodian had a lightened work load. People do want to help. Sometimes all that is needed is to ask them.

IDEA: Utilize parents to work on church projects while they wait for their children to finish choir practice.

One idea that works well is to utilize the assistance of mothers and fathers to work on special church projects while waiting for their sons and daughters to finish choir practice. In many cases, the parents need to drive their kids to church anyway, so they are often glad to lend a hand for an hour or two. The projects could include stuffing envelopes, updating church records, helping with a mailing, making some phone calls, or any task that requires some extra help beyond normal church staff. Are you making use of your choir moms and dads?

IDEA: Use the power of existing groups to tackle new projects.

Chances are your congregation contains many different groups such as circles, regular classes, councils, committees, and clubs. One church used all these groups and others to do a major community project. The church made a one-year commitment to feed the homeless at a local church shelter once per month. They asked twelve established groups within the church to serve a meal per month. Volunteers included a confirmation class, the church council, the young adults group, a Bible study group, and others. Each participating group received the satisfaction of being able to contribute toward a major project. And the individuals within each group got to know each other better as they worked together. Is there a cause in your community that can be tackled by uniting the groups within your church?

IDEA: Train your teachers and volunteers through a newsletter.

If you're having a hard time scheduling a workshop or seminar for your Sunday school or confirmation teachers, why not train them through a newsletter? A short one-page newsletter, written by the pastor or parish education director, could give classroom teaching tips or helpful lesson planning notes on each week's lesson. This not only saves time, but is a quick nonthreatening way to pass on helpful advice and build confidence and enthusiasm in your volunteer teachers.

IDEA: Try using team-teaching for your educational classes.

Several churches use team-teaching for their Sunday school or Christian education classes. The two teachers alternate teaching the same class either week by week or month by month. While many people hesitate to make a full year commitment to teach, this allows for continuity in the classroom while it gives teachers flexibility in scheduling. It also reduces teacher stress, burnout, and can even provide an instant substitute teacher as the other team-teacher can be contacted in case of illness or other emergency.

IDEA: Spread responsibility for church social events to all existing church groups.

A re you having trouble with people in your church getting burned out by planning and implementing too many social events with too little help? One church had a social committee that planned all church social events and the burnout rate was high. Instead of trying to recruit more people to their social ministry team, the committee decided to disband and try something new. Now all church events are the responsibility of all existing church groups. In the beginning of each year, all the different events are assigned to circles, council committees, choirs, and youth groups who each plan and implement the special event they are assigned during the year. One event per group per year is quite manageable for everyone and increases involvement in planning church activities.

WORKING SMARTER

IDEA: Transform your answering machine into an information hotline.

Though some people prefer private confession to talking to answering machines, these electronic message-takers can be used as information-givers as well. They can be turned on Sunday morning or during the week after hours with a message of church service times and a number to call in case of emergency. They can also be used during staff meetings or prayer times to avoid interruptions. You might want to use it as an information hotline to announce upcoming church or youth activities.

IDEA: Create a guide for selecting hymns for church services.

Do you ever find yourself struggling to select a hymn that is both familiar to the congregation and pertinent to your message? One way to avoid this dilemma is to have the organist or choir director go through the hymnal you use, listing by topic (e.g., opening hymns, pulpit hymns, Advent hymns, and so on) those songs known and loved by your members. It's not only helpful for choosing hymns for the service, but is a quick guide for others who plan or help with worship.

IDEA: Compile all wedding options in a single pamphlet.

If you grapple with trying to make a wedding service personal enough for the married couple, and yet orthodox enough for yourself, a convenient solution may be a wedding booklet. It could combine all the best wedding service hymns, scripture readings, vows, blessings, and "extras" in a single source. You include what you feel is appropriate, and indicate what is and isn't optional. The couple then looks over the booklet at their convenience, making notes of the options they want—for example, which of the six vows they want to recite and where they want the solos. They get involved in the process and you receive a ready-made order of service.

IDEA: Use a wedding coordinator to help couples implement weddings.

I f you want to free up your pastor for other things, consider using a wedding coordinator. This is a person who assists the couple in their wedding plans, rehearsal, and details on the day of the ceremony. A coordinator can be a wonderful help for discussing fees, wedding policies at the church, and for giving the pastor some free time on the weekends.

WORSHIP

IDEA: Include a pledge to worship with your financial pledge.

When people are asked to make a yearly pledge to the church, a financial pledge comes to mind. While some churches are now including pledges for volunteer time and use of talents, there is one other pledge that your members can make. One church asks members to make a written pledge to worship a certain number of days per year. This is done the same time financial pledges are made. It keeps track of the worship pledge through Sunday sign-in books. Members are told how they are doing with their worship pledge when they are mailed their financial pledge updates. One advantage of asking for worship pledges is that it helps keep financial pledges current. When members attend church, they usually contribute financially.

IDEA: Highlight the talents of members at services.

If you want to call attention to the many talents and gifts of your church members, focus on talent during a special church service. One way to do this is by having a person with a different talent carry a banner into the sanctuary during the Sunday morning processional. On Easter Sunday, banners were carried to the front of one church sanctuary by a choir member, a council member, a Sunday school teacher, a custodian, an audio-visual person, an usher, and a stewardship team member. Names can be listed in the Sunday bulletin.

IDEA: Use families to participate in worship services.

While churches encourage family worship, others also encourage family participation in the worship service. In Advent, for example, an entire family gathers around the Advent wreath—one person lights the candle while another explains the candle's significance for the season. For Christmas, a family dresses up for the worship service's live manger scene. For communion, an entire family brings forward the bread and wine. These family activities highlight the togetherness of the body of believers.

IDEA: Increase your sensitivity to the comfort and challenges faced by some members during worship services.

It is often easy to have the same expectations for everyone during worship services. We forget that not everyone can hear, some have trouble seeing, and for others, just rising is a challenge. For example, the words "will the congregation please rise" can be a difficult expectation for the elderly. Some churches substitute "please rise as you are able" as more appropriate wording. Having large-print hymnals is also helpful. And have you ever thought of reserving some back pews for latecomers so they do not disrupt the service? Ask members for other ideas on how your church can be more sensitive!

IDEA: Personalize printed materials and educational sessions with favorite Bible verses from members.

Most Christians have favorite Bible verses that when shared can add personalization to printed materials or educational sessions within your church. Why not collect member favorites and use them in the monthly newsletter, on a classroom blackboard, or to start off a meeting? How about placing a favorite verse on a banner or use it to open a Bible study? A member's name, along with the verse, can add a new dimension to their participation.

WRITING

IDEA: Share your ideas and insights with others by submitting sermons and articles for publication.

Have you ever written an article for the weekly church newsletter you just knew was good enough to be published? Or have you preached a sermon so good you thought the rest of the world should hear it? Or perhaps you have some funny anecdote or serious concern you want to share with others? Duane Newcomb gives you the tips, insights, and confidence to get published in his book *How to Sell & Re-Sell Your Writing* (Cincinnati, Ohio: Writer's Digest Books, 1987). Not only is it comprehensive, but it also begins with the basics and progresses logically from scouting out markets, to writing, to selling. Some of your sermons may be ready to be published just as they are! Find out if there is a freelance writer within you!

IDEA: Use grid paper when laying out a flyer or newsletter.

If staff or volunteers find it difficult to align clip art or headlines for the weekly bulletin or newsletter, grid paper can solve the difficulty. Grid paper has light blue guidelines and is designed to make layout easier. The grid squares, which are a quarter of an inch across, allow easy setup for any cut-and-paste operation such as headlines, drawings, or clip art. Best of all, the lines do not show up when the page is duplicated on a copier. The grid paper is also excellent for freehand announcements or posters.

IDEA: Use these two ways to be sure headlines or art work are level on a page.

Sometimes it is tough to get art work or a headline level on a page. No matter how hard you try, what looks level to the eye can be quite a bit crooked or off-center. There are two ways to "get it straight" the first time. Photocopy the page and then fold it in half. If the headline or art is level, the left and right sides of the art or copy will touch when folded in half. (Only a line that is level on a piece of paper will have both ends meet when folded.) Another method you can use is to place the paper or page in question at your feet and look down on it. The distance helps you see whether the copy or art was placed straight or not.

IDEA: Utilize the mailing area of your newsletter to print an advertisement or important message.

What's the most important event that is happening at your church this month? Why not utilize the mailing area on an envelope or in your newsletter to print a five- or six-word headline that conveys a brief reminder of it? The headline should be placed just below the mailing label. Some churches do this every month in their newsletter and highlight one event. Example: (Church Dinner Is December 12. See page 3). It is sure to be noticed and is a low-cost way of getting your message across.

IDEA: Create an outline in five easy steps.

The next time you have to write a talk or presentation in a hurry, create a thorough outline in these five easy steps: (1) state the topic, (2) write down the main point or conclusion, (3) create an attention-getting opening, (4) name your major points, and (5) support each major point with two or three short sentences.

IDEA: Create an area of interest to your Sunday school children in your church newsletter.

Here's an idea on how to make your church newsletter more "colorful" and have it reach a new audience. One church newsletter has a "Children's Corner" designed for younger readers. Some months it has a picture that can be colored, or else an easy-to-do activity like a quiz or puzzle. This idea increases the feeling of "belonging" to young members and gives them something to look forward to when the newsletter arrives.

IDEA: If you are having trouble writing something and experience "writer's block," try a more flexible approach.

When words don't flow, learn to be flexible. First, go back and write a general outline of what you want to write. Second, begin with the area with which you feel most comfortable. If you can't think of an introduction, skip it entirely or simply write down the gist of the paragraph, then move on to the next one. If it means starting in the middle of your article or even with your conclusion, begin there. And if you simply can't think of an outline that makes sense, begin writing and come up with an outline after you've finished. Although this may sound backwards, there are advantages. It gets you writing rather than frustrated, it provides direction, and it keeps you organized. Keep these ideas in mind and you'll never be at a loss for words!

IDEA: Try these simple tips to improve your newsletter.

If you want to improve how your newsletter looks and gain readership, try some of these suggestions: (1) eliminate vague headlines, and utilize verbs and dates of events—some people may read just the headline, nothing else; (2) put important copy in bold—some people just skim articles, so let them know what's important; (3) remind readers to remove the calendar from their newsletter and post it where it will be noticed; and (4) utilize the mailing area on a newsletter for simple messages and headlines.

IDEA: Spice up church publications to increase participation.

Gain a greater reading audience for your church publications by adding puzzles, anecdotes, or pictures. Crossword puzzles, word scrambles, and photos add interest for people who might not otherwise read the publication. It also provides a more personal, engaging format that enhances the written word and sets a mood of interest and enjoyment. Think about it for yourself. Would you rather look at a picture or a page bulging with text?

YOUTH

IDEA: Reward classroom participation with cards.

Have you ever had a problem getting members of a confirmation class to share ideas or answers during a discussion? One way to motivate participation is to give out single cards such as sports collectibles as rewards for contributions. The participant with the most variety at the end of class earns a small prize. Your class members will be motivated to get involved and will enjoy comparing and collecting the cards with their classmates.

IDEA: To bring reality to teaching, try going on location.

For your next Bible study or confirmation class, why not try it on location? If you are talking about Golgotha, pile the youth in a car and take them to the nearest garbage dump. Tell a parable in a boat, pushed away from shore. Is there a private garden around to substitute for Gethsemane or the Garden of Eden? A trip to a Jewish synagogue can add some real insights also.

IDEA: Ask class participants to draw a picture of what they have learned.

If your confirmation class needs a change of pace, ask participants to describe the two most important points they have just learned by drawing a picture of each concept. Collect all the drawings and ask the class to guess the points that are represented. Allow time for each artist to say a few words, too.

IDEA: Assign an adult to be a mentor to a confirmation student.

How do you make the Christian faith real to ninth grade confirmation students? One way is to assign an adult member of the congregation to be their "mentor." The mentor and the student do social things together, act as study partners, and learn from each other how to be a disciple of Jesus Christ. This technique has been so successful in some churches, mentors have become a regular part of the last year of confirmation.

IDEA: Have sixth graders become pals with senior citizens.

At a prayer retreat for sixth graders, one church gave each youth the name of a shut-in or senior citizen. The sixth graders were then asked to write a short note to their older friends, telling them they were praying for them. The youth had a chance to experience intercessory prayer firsthand, the seniors were touched in a powerful way (some were moved to tears), and both groups had a cross-generational pen pal.

IDEA: Give class credit for church camp experiences.

Church and Bible camps can offer some of the most memorable faith experiences young people ever have. There is concentrated time for building relationships with adult counselors, other believers, and a recommitment to faith. For these reasons, several churches give Sunday school or confirmation credit for camp and retreat experiences. For example, a weekend retreat is worth four hours of class time. A week-long camp is good for eight hours of class. This provides an enjoyable learning opportunity for youth while it allows you to shape the experience to your curriculum concerns.

IDEA: Youth can make personalized cards as gifts for parents.

One unique gift idea for Sunday school or confirmation classes is for the participants to make cards for their parents at

Christmas or for Mother's Day, Father's Day, or Thanksgiving. While the outside of the card may look like any other, it is the inside that makes each card so original. Each student writes the things they have appreciated most about their parents. They could write these or similar words: "These are the things you have given me as parents that have made me who I am today. . ." The students then list happy moments, remembered events, or treasured times together as the gifts they have received in the past. It can also be a good discussion starter for homes where kids do not feel appreciated or loved, focusing on human imperfection and God's unconditional love.

IDEA: Use volleyball as a recreational function for young adults.

For over seven years, one church has been involved in an exciting young adult ministry that has enriched the congregation. Every Wednesday, young adults ages eighteen to thirty-nine get together to play volleyball. This is followed by fellowship and a faith discussion group. People are encouraged to bring friends and utilize teamwork in the games. During the winter, the games move to a gym. This way of bringing young adults to the church is virtually without expense and requires only a place to play and someone to show up with the equipment. A number of young adults ended up joining the church and becoming active members because a friend invited them to volleyball. Several marriages have even resulted. If you are looking for inexpensive programming that really makes an impact, consider volleyball.

IDEA: Give youth a tour of little-known places in their city.

One youth group makes an annual event of touring little-known "hot spots" in their city. They first load up cars and head off to a park to fly kites. They give each team a kite, string, and rags, and then the race is on to see who can get the kite off the ground first. Then they pile into cars and go to a go-cart track with a fast-pitch batting cage. From there they go visit the oldest house in the city, a small museum, and the day ends at a hole-in-the-wall café that has the best greasy cheeseburgers in town. It's an inexpensive, but memorable afternoon.

THE CHURCH IDEA BOOK

IDEA: Look for three-hour service projects for youth within your town.

Instead of looking for youth or adult service projects in Mexico, New York, or Alaska, why not begin at home? A young adult group from one church gathered the names of widows or seniors from their own congregation that needed house and yard work done. They spent a few hours cleaning, painting, and raking leaves. Not only did they find that the opportunities were plentiful, but they also developed new friendships and sensitivity at the same time.

IDEA: Schedule a youth retreat during the school week as many schools have policies that permit it as an excused absence.

Many schools still offer "comp" time for students participating in religious education or other church activities. One church takes advantage of this by scheduling a day-long confirmation retreat once a year during the school week. Since it follows the schedule of a regular class day, students can take the bus to and from school as usual and partake in after-school activities. The youth enjoy the different setting, and because it is an excused absence, 100 percent class attendance is nearly guaranteed.

IDEA: Bring youth and parents together for confirmation registration and orientation by scheduling a fun night.

Instead of pulling teeth to get parents and youth together for confirmation registration and orientation, one church uses a fun night to highlight the event. People gather an hour early for an informal dinner, registering and filling out the necessary paperwork at their convenience. After dinner, both parents and youth gather for questions, concerns, and information about upcoming educational sessions. A half hour later, the parents discuss special concerns while the youth go off to enjoy games and mixers led by adults. The whole event, which can be done in less than two hours, promotes fellowship as well as support for concerned and harried parents.

IDEA: Use your favorite video to promote the gospel to youth.

A confirmation teacher used a secular video to proclaim the message of Christmas. She accomplished this during Advent by showing "How the Grinch Stole Christmas." Points were awarded to each of two teams when they made a connection between the video and Luke's Christmas account (e.g., a bright star appeared in Whoville just as it appeared in Bethlehem). The exercise promoted both creativity and excitement for the biblical story.

COMMUNICATION

Share the Feeling

The subject had come up before at the church council meeting. In fact, it had come up several times, but nothing had been done—handicap parking at the church was inadequate. The situation changed, however, when Joan addressed the council with her concerns and frustrations. Pointing to her own leg cast, she gave a firsthand account about the difficulty and inconvenience of current handicap parking. Her heartfelt plea forced the council to see the issue on a personal level, and additional signs and space for handicap parking were added the next day.

Our feelings tell people where we are in an open, honest way. You can't argue with feelings, because it's not a majority vote—only one person knows what he or she is feeling. Our feelings are also nonjudgmental; they don't make claims on others, but simply express what we're experiencing. It's also healthy to share what's churning up our insides; once we've said what we're feeling, we are free to focus on a solution rather than fume over the problem.

We need not wait to share feelings as a last resort, when they will more likely erupt with negative, self-defeating consequences.

Where or how can you use feelings as an aid for ministry?

1. To clarify communication (e.g., "I'm a little confused. . ." or "I feel like I haven't been clear. . .")

2. To clarify ministry with volunteers (e.g., "Sara, how are you feeling about this position? Do you feel supported?")

3. To get at the pulse of the congregation (e.g., "John, I sense frustration in the congregation—how are you feeling about how things are going?")

4. To help explain your view of ministry to others (e.g., "I'm feeling slightly overwhelmed with the meetings, expectations, and after-hour calls.")

A flower ad reads, "Turn feelings into flowers." Sharing feelings can be a healthy approach for getting positive results.

CREATIVE CHRISTIANITY

Implementing New Ideas

A re you tired of having some things done the same way year after year at your church? Is it time for some changes?

If you are looking for new approaches for being more creative in your ministry (or you want to try something new at your church), it's time to throw away some rules and take a fresh look at your world. Here are some proven techniques for generating ideas within your church.

1. Ask "Why?" Unleash your curiosity concerning the current situation. For example, why is your church newsletter printed in the same format month after month? Or why is the annual church report always in written form only? You'll find that many activities and functions are the same year after year simply because they have always been done that way. How many things can you list at your church that are the same every year? Is the original reason still valid, or is it time for a change?

2. Remember that there is more than one right answer. If you think there is only one correct solution to any problem, you are being kept from considering other solutions. Don't halt your search for ideas just because you have one answer. Come up with another.

3. Act fast. When a new idea hits, act on it while you still have the passion to accomplish it. At the very least, write the idea on paper so that you don't forget it.

4. Fight for your ideas. If you have a good idea, promote it with enthusiasm. Stick with it. Did you know that the inventors of flypaper were two high school boys who were almost laughed out of town?

5. Get the facts about your subject. Knowledge is powerful. Study and learn all you can about what you want to accomplish. Ask questions of others who may be able to help you in your search.

6. Learn from failures. Don't be afraid to make mistakes; they can be rich opportunities for learning. If one proposed solution fails, give it up and try another approach.

7. Give new twists to old ideas. A chunk of rubber wallpaper cleaner inspired the idea of an eraser at the end of a pencil. And the idea for typewriter keys came from the keys on a piano. Think of what can be updated and reapplied to a new situation or circumstance at your church.

8. Focus on human needs. Your creativity is best directed at solving problems within your church. What gripes do members have? What's inconvenient? What problem occurs every year? Use these as a starting point for creative solutions.

CREATIVITY

Consume Yourself

In her marvelous book *If You Want to Write,* Brenda Ueland talks about the need to lose oneself when working or writing. She says that the tragedy of so-called worthless people is that "they perhaps have more thoughts than us rushers, but they never get them out on paper or canvas or in music or work because of . . . self-doubt, fear of failure, and so on.

"Another trouble with writers in the first twenty years," she continues, "is an anxiety to be effective, to impress people. They write pretentiously." See *If You Want to Write* (St. Paul, Minn.: Graywolf Press, 1987), pp. 59 and 63.

Ueland's theory is that the very standards that strive to make us successful unintentionally stymie our creativity. The pressure to meet quotas and deadlines and expectations edges out our creative impulses and replaces them with the shallow criteria that only satisfies others.

The solution? Let your work consume you. Get involved fully in what you are doing. Let your instinct take you where it will. Go for a ride with your ingenuity. Give God the room to use all of you. Dare to do what you do that makes you *you,* rather than what makes you an image of what others expect.

Teach as though nothing else matters. Preach as though you believe your words are able to give life. Visit as though the most important person is the one who sits before you. Write as though your thoughts and feelings and instincts can transform lives through the power of God. Let your work consume you rather than control you.

Your creative genius lies within you, not within someone else. So why not use it? Consume yourself and see what happens.

DECISIONS AND
BOILING POINTS

"**I**'m sorry, the owner can't talk to you at the moment, can I take a message?" a voice asked on the other line, minus any sentiment or concern.

"No, I'll wait, thank you."

"Well, you can wait if you'd like, Mr. Groth, but he may not be free for several hours. I suggest you call back at a later time. . . ."

"I've already called back at later times," I hissed, "five later times, and it hasn't worked. Tell Mr. Jeffreys I'd like to speak to him personally about getting a new modem. This is the third time I've brought it in for repair."

I had reached my boiling point. I felt as though I was being ignored, as though my concerns were trivial and unimportant. Hadn't anybody listened to me over the past two weeks? No more Mr. Nice Guy. I had been flexible long enough.

If the truth were to be known, I had been flexible too long. In fact, that was precisely the cause of my dilemma. Who was going to help a customer that had the patience of Job when other customers needed help immediately? Of course I needed immediate help as well, I just hadn't conveyed it clearly enough—that is, until my system could no longer take it. It was get angry or get an ulcer.

Unfortunately, this is how most of us make decisions. Whether it's being flexible or organized or sympathetic or unrealistic or passive, most of us make the majority of our decisions using one strategy or strength. In other words, we have found a "strength" that works for us in most situations. If organization gives us security, we will make decisions that are organized. If procrastination works, we will procrastinate. Our strength is whatever works for us in making decisions.

While none of these "strengths" are good or bad in themselves, the rub is that we'll use the same strength over and over again, even though circumstances differ greatly. But like using a sledgehammer to put up a thumbtack, our strength doesn't always match the situation. But we go ahead and use that eight-pound mallet until we go through the wall and are forced to take out a tinker's hammer! More often than not, we allow the situation to dictate our actions, rather than vice versa.

How much better it would be if we acted differently before the situation forced us to reach our boiling point. How much better (and more honest) it would have been for me to be inflexible and unyielding about my defective computer modem two weeks earlier. How much better for Mr. Jeffreys and his employees! It would have saved a lot of hard feelings and misunderstandings.

It doesn't have to be that way, however. We can change strategies before we are backed into a corner. How can you deal with decision-making problems?

1. Decide what your "strength" is in making decisions. Are you flexible? Realistic? Optimistic? Detail oriented? Task oriented? Good at procrastinating?

2. When making future decisions, ask if this is an appropriate time to use your strength. Will another method work better in this particular circumstance?

3. If you have made a decision by reaching the "boiling point," ask yourself if you could have made the decision earlier, before the situation forced you to act.

4. Think of how you make decisions in your relationships outside the church (e.g., spouse, friend). Would other options work in these relationships as well?

5. Look at the way other people make decisions. Are they helpful or harmful? What can you incorporate into your own decision-making system that would make it more productive and increase your options?

EVALUATION

How Am I Doing?

I recently conducted an adult forum at our church with a woman who worked for the school district. We had both presented material on the topic of Satanism, she from her viewpoint as a chemical health coordinator, and me from the spiritual viewpoint. After we had finished the two one-hour sessions, she asked to my surprise, "So, when are we going to sit down and evaluate how we did?"

The question caught me off-guard for several reasons. First, we were evaluating a one-hour presentation, which almost seemed too short to evaluate. Second, we were not planning on doing the forum again—I generally tie evaluations to repeat performances. Third, she said it so casually that I was sure that she did evaluations as a matter of course while I did them only when I had to. And fourth, her attitude was so positive I couldn't help but think it would be a good experience. And it was.

I have had to rethink my position on evaluations since then. After completing a four-week Bible study for our congregation, the other pastors and I were curious about how things went. Did the lecturing format work well? How did the people like the study guide? Was the sound system clear? Were the overhead transparencies meaningful? Did we cover too much material in too short a time? Was there enough opportunity to look up references in the Bible? Would the group like to cover similar material in the future? As we continued to talk I found it difficult to contain myself. "We should have an evaluation form," I blurted out.

I was as surprised as the rest of them to hear such words spew forth. But you could tell by their gestures and silence that they, too, could see the light.

The fruits of evaluation can be reaped anytime. Take a few minutes to ask if the following or similar questions could pay back big dividends in the future. Here they are:
- What was your objective?
- Did you meet your desired goals?

- How did the audience respond? Were they perceptive? Annoyed? Delighted? Shocked?
- How did your own presentation go?
- What did you do well? What did others appreciate?
- Where could you improve?
- Were the physical surroundings comfortable?
- Was the atmosphere conducive to your objectives?
- If mechanical aids were used, did they work well? Would a substitute work better?

FAMILY GROUPS

A Way for Strangers to Become Friends

Were there strangers in your church last Sunday? Perhaps they weren't first-time guests, but rather church members who knew few, if any, other people. It's a problem common to most congregations—members do not know each other.

While the desire to build friendships and Christian relationships is strong, it's tough to strike up a conversation with a stranger. It's even tougher to turn an acquaintance into a close friend, especially when time is limited to a few minutes between services. Family groups are a way to make friends within the church in a relaxed setting while providing the "connection" many members seek. It's an opportunity for face-to-face fellowship, a time to be open and share dreams and fears in an accepting, risk-free environment.

A family group consists of four to twelve church members who get together on a regular basis (weekly or twice a month) for the purpose of becoming better acquainted with one another. The group meets in the homes of members for about two hours per meeting. Time, day, and location are set by the participants.

Family groups promote individual as well as spiritual growth. Meetings include time for sharing, prayer, and fellowship. A leader facilitates each meeting, and can offer questions for discussion. Participants share as they desire.

Although the Bible can be utilized, sharing personal experiences and feelings is just as important in this context as biblical knowledge. The textbook is human life. People grow from the give-and-take of real life experiences, as well as from the word of God.

Format
A family group meeting can include the following:
- Welcome by the leader
- Discussion of the group's purpose
- Opening prayer
- Discussion of a topic
- Time for individual sharing about the past week

- Prayer concerns
- Refreshments
- Future planning

A group might want to schedule an entire meeting strictly for socializing. The participants could meet at a pizza parlor, go bowling, have a potluck at a home, play board games, or attend a movie together.

Topics

The discussion topic could change weekly or remain the same for six to eight weeks. Here are some possibilities: prayer, communication, witnessing, death, ethics, values, minorities, other religions, faith, or friendship.

Whatever topic you select, it can serve as a catalyst for members to get to know each other better through continuing discussions. The commitment to talk on a regular basis forms lasting relationships.

Benefits

Family groups offer several advantages. The organization is minimal. There is no cost. People of all ages can participate. And the results are immediate: members have friends to talk to and people to sit with during services. It's a nice way for the church to get behind the faces and into the hearts of some of their members.

How to Start a Family Group

1. Make it simple and informal.
2. Select a topic and a discussion leader.
3. Explain the family group concept in the Sunday bulletin.
4. Announce starting and ending dates for the sessions.
5. Create a registration form and obtain commitments.

GROUPS

Getting Them to Help You

It is shortly after 8:00 P.M. on January 11, and your small aircraft has crash-landed just north of the Canadian border. Though the crew members have been killed, you are among the handful of survivors that have sustained minor injuries. You are fifty miles from the nearest city and have decided to stay together as a group. First, however, you must decide which items aboard the plane are most crucial for your survival.

So begins one of the many group survival games used to aid groups in making decisions. Each participant individually rates the twenty survival items in order of decreasing importance, and then repeats the exercise as a member of a group. Each correct answer receives five points. When the scores are tallied and those of the individuals are compared to those of the larger group, the results are consistently the same. If there are no "experts" (in this case a survival expert), groups will consistently score higher than any single individual. In fact, decisions by group consensus typically score 30 to 50 percent higher than those of individuals.

Group consensus can be a healthy and beneficial source of information. Each person brings a background of skills and knowledge that can inform and direct the decision-making process in a positive way (if we decide to use them, that is!). Here are a few suggestions to change your next meeting into a learning opportunity.

Use the knowledge of others for your benefit. Pretend that you are a novice in the subject, and begin by asking questions. This does two things. First, it takes the pressure away from being the expert. Second, it invites others to share their own ideas. You can then add your "expert" opinion when it helps to clarify or affirm points made in the discussion.

Look at ideas as neutral. Too often we defend our points of view because we see their endorsement as an acceptance of who we are as people. In other words, when people accept our idea, we feel good about ourselves because it shows that we are creative thinkers. Look at ideas as neutral; be able to give them the third degree yourself. Look at them as something to examine, rather than something capable of boosting or deflating your ego.

Encourage differing viewpoints. Agreement doesn't always mean something is right, especially in the church. Diverse perspectives give us an opportunity to point out the variety in the body of believers. Get disagreements out in the open, where they can be dealt with, rather than playing hide-and-seek with them later.

Respond to feelings. Words and sentences are only one medium of communication and can often camouflage the true feelings of others. If messages appear mixed or confused, try to identify the emotion behind the statements. It could be a useful starting point for clarification (e.g., "Hazel, I sense you're angry with what's just been said. . . .").

IRRIGATING CHURCH SWAMPS

One day in class, I was impressed with a marvelous thought by E. Cotton Mather, a wise geography professor known around the world for his innovative thinking. He was discussing the ramifications of water irrigation and said something like this: "Why is it that people spend millions of dollars irrigating the desert to grow crops? Why not drain a swamp instead? Deserts are dry and are not conducive to retaining water moisture. Swamps, on the other hand, are wonderful for retaining moisture. After the initial draining, the irrigation process is natural; the soil is continually moist."

I have thought often about the wisdom of Professor Mather's proposal. It's simplicity is disarming. The message that still stands out for me is, "keep the natural natural. Use the existing system to your advantage. Let it help you, rather than hinder you, using as little energy as possible."

Are there swamps at your church that can be drained and irrigated? Are there messy situations currently in front of you that you could use to your advantage, rather than disadvantage? What systems are in place that you can use in a positive way?

The Youth Scholarship Committee at church was planning a date for a fund raiser to build the coffer for college and seminary scholarships. A few dates were suggested, but these conflicted with the meeting times of other church groups, one of which was the church council. Suddenly I saw a church swamp that could be drained.

"Why not have the fund raiser the same night as the church council meeting?" I asked. "They are a strong supporter for what we are doing. They already have a meeting that night, so they don't have to block out another night for yet another commitment. Besides, they'd only have to postpone their meeting twenty minutes. We'd also have a captive audience who would be given an easy opportunity to help us. And best of all, since half of us are on the church council, we wouldn't have to schedule an additional night to meet either."

It was a wonderful idea. I sat smugly, face illumined, waiting for the wisdom to permeate the room. It didn't take long before someone answered. "How about scheduling the fund raiser a week AFTER the church council meets?"

Though draining church swamps can get a little murky at times, it's well worth the effort. Yes, even if others would rather irrigate deserts.

MANAGEMENT

Keeping Your Leaders Out in the Lead

If the toilets in your church plug up, who is the first person contacted? If youth are having a quarrel outside, or if someone needs to know where to sign up for the coed softball league, or if Martha's mom needs directions to the Sunday school class, or if an usher is sick and needs a substitute, or if the coffeepot stops working (or worse yet, the coffee hasn't been made and it's fifteen minutes before the social hour begins), to whom do people turn? While the pastor is an obvious choice, it isn't always convenient to engage his or her services as a plumber two minutes before the worship service begins.

Below are a few ways other churches have kept their leaders out in the open so that the business of the church can be conducted quickly and efficiently, letting pastors do what they were called to do.

Print the names of church leaders in the bulletin. Display the names of council members, elders, church presidents, Christian education directors, and others in a prominent place. Why not list them on the cover of the bulletin?

Make permanent name tags for church leaders. Color-coded name tags are an easy way to identify and distinguish the ushers from the Sunday school teachers and from the custodial staff. Encourage people to wear these name tags to church social events as well. They are there to serve the church, not to remain in hiding.

Feature church leaders regularly in the church publication or newsletter. Include photos, hobbies, interests, and descriptions of your leaders. You might also try highlighting your leaders through regular columns or interviews in the church newsletter.

MANAGEMENT

Managing Your Environment

As an identical twin, I have been involved in a lifelong debate over the importance of heredity and environment. I have discovered that while nothing can be done about genetic makeup, a change in environment can do wonders.

Former Minnesota governor Elmer Anderson indicated the same when he recently addressed a group of pastors. One of his challenges to the ministry was to "create environments where people can be their best."

What is the office environment like at your church? Below are several working areas where you can be intentional about bringing out the best in others.

Office Staff Area

What is the atmosphere like for staff and visitors? Is it open and welcome? Is there room for flexibility and change and creativity? Does the environment encourage communication and discussion? Is there a forum or method for suggestions and disagreements? Does the staff feel supported, respected, and trusted?

Personal Office

Does your office or work area energize and give you direction and reason for action? Does it reflect your faith or motivation? Is it an atmosphere that ignites your enthusiasm? Perhaps you need a quote, a picture, or music playing softly in the background to reflect and encourage values and goals.

Desk Area

"Cluttered desk, cluttered mind," may be more than just a nice aphorism. Paul Borthwick discusses "environmental management" for the desktop in his book, *Organizing Your Youth Ministry*. The following may help to keep your own desk uncluttered, whether you're using an organized system or the "put it anywhere" system.

1. Keep only one project on your desk at a time. Other projects should be filed or stored elsewhere until you are ready for them.

2. Complete the project in front of you before moving on, no matter how attractive or tempting the next project may be.

3. Avoid unnecessary interruptions. Take your breaks or visit after you've finished the task completely.

4. If you delegate the project to others, record the necessary details of who, when, and where—then jot down a date on your calendar for follow-up.

5. Recheck your priorities and move on to the next important project.

Office Products and Equipment

The Rhode Island Solid Waste Management Corporation suggests many helpful ways to manage and unclutter the larger office work environment while saving dollars in the process. Some of their suggestions:

- Purchase maintenance contracts to extend the life of your current equipment.
- Sell or donate your old equipment so that it ends up in the hands of others, rather than in a landfill.
- Check with your copy machine service representative about "recharging" the used cartridge rather than buying a new one—it could save you up to half the cost.
- Copy documents on both sides of the paper. Remember to do the same when sending materials out to be printed.
- Edit documents as much as possible on the computer screen. Double check drafts before making copies.
- Bind your used office paper printed on one side only (e.g., computer printouts, memos, and so on) for memo pads, note pads, or work pads. These can be cut to desired sizes.
- Save interoffice envelopes, manila envelopes, and file folders for future use.
- Do away with unnecessary forms. Circulate, rather than copy, necessary messages or forms whenever possible.
- Maintain mailing lists and church membership lists to cut down on duplications and extra mailing costs.
- Provide coffee mugs and glasses for employees and visitors rather than disposable cups.
- Save reusable goods and donate to a local charity.

You do more than simply exist in an environment; you help create it. Why not use it to bring out the best in your ministry and the ministry of others?

MANAGEMENT

User Fees

I was looking over the fees our church charged for weddings to couples who were nonmembers. The fee for our secretary to type and photocopy 100 bulletins was $5.00. "Marge," I asked, "how long does it take you just to type up one of these wedding services?"

"Well," she said, "it depends on how legible the original information sheet is and how many times I have to call the couple for information. Once I get all the details, it takes about a half hour to an hour."

"And how much do we need to charge just to break even on the photocopies?" I continued.

"About a nickel a piece," was her reply.

My curiosity was getting the best of me. "And how do we charge for the bulletins?"

"We charge the couple what the publisher charges us, except we pick up the postage."

I quickly scanned the list for other fees. Fifty dollars for using the sanctuary in a million-dollar complex. Five dollars for the use of fourteen specially made beeswax candles, which had to be tossed after two or three uses. Five dollars for using the silver serving set. Fifty dollars for the pastor, which included five to eight hours of premarital counseling, the wedding rehearsal, and several hours on the day of the wedding.

It didn't take long to see that our church was losing money when performing these wedding services to nonmembers. And since the majority of these couples had no interest in the church, but were merely church shopping (about one in seven joined the church after the nuptial services), it didn't seem to be much of a ministry.

I thank Lyle Schaller for raising the concept of "user fees" in his book *44 Ways to Expand the Financial Base of Your Congregation* (Nashville: Abingdon Press, 1989). While Schaller does not jump on one side of the fence or the other in charging user fees, he raises some of the key issues in the debate of charging for services offered in the church. Should we charge Sunday school children for the cost of materials and work books? Should we charge community groups for the use of the facilities? Should we charge members to help offset some of the expenses offered in special programming?

The idea of the user fee is to pass on all or part of the cost of the service to those benefiting directly from the service. When you go to a state park, you pay a user fee. When you go to the municipal swimming pool, you pay a user fee. Some public schools are now charging fees for those who choose to participate in sporting events or band. When user fees are charged, it is the consumer who pays for the services they receive.

But user fees also raise some serious theological questions. What is the ministry of the church in providing services to others? How do these fees relate to God's unbounded love and the free gift of grace? If members are already supporting the church through financial gifts, how can we charge them again for services they receive? Is this in keeping with our basic beliefs about stewardship? And why are we charging such fees? Is it to further the ministry of the church, or to merely enhance the bottom line?

In making a decision on whether or not to charge a user fee, thinking about some of the following issues may prove helpful.

1. For both members and nonmembers, will people feel more of a commitment to the activity if charged? They usually do.

2. What is the going rate for the same service in the community? Should a church offering a first-rate day care program charge less simply because it is run by the church?

3. What does the church pay to keep the space available? What does it cost to recoup expenses in terms of lighting, air conditioning, water, garbage, sewer, and so forth? It may be helpful to come up with a cost estimate per square foot of the building.

4. For members, is it possible to charge for materials only? While the church budget covers salaries and the church building, it doesn't always cover programming expenses. For example, if the church offers a Bible study, you might charge for the books needed (nonbudgeted items) but not for the pastor or the building (budgeted items).

5. Are the services you offer providing the outreach you intend? I've discovered from the nonmember weddings I've done that people are more interested in a bargain than they are in making a commitment to the church. For this reason we've raised our prices for these services. Members pay significantly lower fees.

6. Are there items your church members would gladly cover out of pocket? Our church offering envelopes are given out free, yet each year several hundred are not picked up. What about the church magazine, devotional materials, and Bible tracts? Some members might gladly pick up the bill for such materials.

While the church is in the boat of other nonprofitable organizations, it is a fact that dollars keep it afloat. Our responsibility is to make those dollars cover as much ministry as possible.

MARKETING

Reaching Out Within Your Community

Your church can play a larger role in your community by simply identifying and striving to meet the needs of the people in your neighborhood. There are dozens of ways to begin.

A good place to start is with your current church membership. Asking members how they were introduced to your church (how they happened to attend for the first time) can give you valuable information as to what has worked in the past.

Go public. If you have an active group of singles, senior citizens, or couples, are they open to the public? If so, how can you communicate that nonmembers are welcome?

If your church has a sale or bazaar, why not include a church brochure with each purchase?

Have you ever considered a public newsletter? You probably already have a newsletter that goes to "insiders" or members of the church. A public newsletter, however, could contain neighborhood news along with news about your church that nonmembers would find informative.

Press releases can be an important tool for communicating a message to the general public. Could someone at your church volunteer to send out press releases on a regular basis?

Is there a need for regular neighborhood meetings in the area in which your church is located? Perhaps the focus could be crime prevention or cutting down the use of illegal drugs. If your church takes the lead by offering a friendly meeting place for this or other activities, it could be the start of a rewarding ministry.

MEETINGS

Keeping on Schedule

To keep a meeting on schedule doesn't require a miracle from God, but it does need the cooperation of the participants. Some of the following might prove helpful to keep you and your committees on track.

1. Agree to and stick to a starting time and an ending time. Lunchtime or quitting time provides a good time to break.

2. Cover priority topics first, starting with the most important. Even if you run out of time, you'll have accomplished something.

3. Distribute handouts before the meeting begins. Have the participants read and consider material prior to sitting down together. Not only does it give more time for members to think about important issues, but it lets them come prepared and informed. Remember, meetings aren't for reading.

4. Identify side issues as they arise. If someone is getting off the track, tactfully point it out to avoid going along for the ride.

5. Bring closure to the meeting. Five or ten minutes before the meeting ends start bringing it to a close by drawing attention to the time. Begin your wrap-up early so that you don't need extra time to close your meeting.

MEETINGS

Ten Ways to Make Them More Effective

Busy church leaders can maximize their effectiveness in many ways, one of which is through conducting and participating in meetings that get the job done. Here are ten ideas for making the most of your meetings.

1. Is a meeting necessary? Before you schedule a meeting, ask if the information that needs to be discussed can be handled better by memo, telephone, or informal conversation. It's also important to be careful not to turn an individual issue between two people into a group meeting. Decide who will benefit before the meeting.

2. Have a written list of objectives. It's wise to distribute your list at least a day in advance. By writing down specific objectives, you increase your chances of eliminating side issues and staying on track. It also helps to consider how much time each issue will take so that you can meet each objective.

3. Evaluate your meetings. How effective are they? Take time to jot down what you like and dislike about them. Is the length appropriate? Are objectives being reached? How could meetings be improved? Ask people for input.

4. Limit the number of participants. Meetings generally are more effective when fewer people are involved. Those who simply need to be informed can be issued a memo after the meeting. Respect other people's time by utilizing them only as necessary.

5. Avoid activity traps. Focus on results. For example, if there is no business for your regular monthly meeting, perhaps it can be postponed until a later date. Regularly scheduled meetings are great for improving communication, but if there is no real business and people are busy, such meetings can waste time and drain personal effectiveness.

6. Do your homework. Before you attend a meeting, review the agenda. Review any material submitted in advance and jot down questions you need answered. Prior preparation can make meetings faster and more effective.

7. Utilize luncheon meetings. It's a great way to satisfy your appetite and accomplish work at the same time. Breakfast meetings are also a good way to get a group together before the activities and challenges of the new day divert their attention.

8. Staff your meetings. It seems silly to mention, but someone should be designated as leader. If the topic is important, one of the participants should take notes. It helps to put in writing the results of the meeting, especially with those doing follow up. Putting decisions on paper gives them a better chance for success.

9. Take breaks as necessary. Breaks not only help you to be more mentally effective, but can also be used as an incentive for accomplishment. Agree to take a break after one or two major decisions are made.

10. Learn to place a value on your time. Consider time spent in a meeting against what you could be doing in your office or elsewhere.

PROGRAMMING FOR NEEDS

What criteria do you use for adding another program at your church? Do you add it because you think it will draw more visitors? Do you add it because you think people want it? Or do you add it because people have expressed a need for the program?

H. Stephen Glenn, community coordinator and nationally known speaker on education, emphasizes focusing on the latter. While people may be attracted to programs initially because of pizzazz or hype, they will only stay in the program if it meets a particular need. If the need isn't met, people will stop coming.

Planning for youth events bears this out. Simply trying to be more creative with our planning to compete with other events vying for youth's time isn't always the key. Undoubtedly the first question youth ask is, "Who else is going?" Youth don't want a great program, they want to have fun with peers they feel comfortable with. They need fellowship. Thinking we'll get youth solely because we're doing something neat misses the mark.

This is especially true in service projects. Youth don't want to spend eight hours on Saturday painting a house because it's fun; they paint it because they feel a need to be needed. They need to know that they can make a difference in the world. And so they paint to fulfill a need, rather than because they want to.

Similarly, people join a Bible study out of a need to build a union with the living Christ, not because they have an extra hour to waste during the week.

Before planning your next program, you may find it helpful to ask yourself first, "What do people need? In what ways can we fulfill those needs?" Doing so should give you a program that is not only well attended, but also one that lasts and continues to generate life into itself.

RECYCLING IN THE OFFICE

Taking care of the environment is good stewardship of both the earth and our monetary resources. Here are a few ways you can begin around the office.

1. Don't toss paper until it's been used on both sides. Save the second side for notes, memos, scratch paper, or next month's church council agenda.

2. Call city or county agencies to check what's available for recycling. Some counties will place large containers in your office area and pick it up when it's full of paper.

3. Bring a mug to work. Better yet, have a supply on hand for office guests.

4. Save manila envelopes received in the mail and reuse them for office communications or storage. Or, get a few labels to cover up the old addresses and send them out a second time.

5. When using the copy machine, copy on both sides if possible. If you only need one side, can you save the paper and reuse the other side for future copies?

6. Keep track of how many copies are made at your church by individuals, groups, and committees. Or start charging committees for each copy made (this can be taken out of their budgeted amount). Simply seeing a numerical count is often shocking enough to think twice about the need for making copies.

7. Have an energy audit to assess your use of electricity at work.

8. Think of the ways you save energy at home and transfer those ideas that can also work at the office.

RITUAL

Helping Faith Feel at Home

I was talking with a small group of people in order to get feedback on what we were and weren't doing right at the church. When the topic of worship came up, one of the women sighed longingly and said, "When are we going to sing those good old hymns? I miss the songs from the other hymnal." As others joined in her lament, it became clear how important music was not only for conveying the presence of God, but also for making people feel comfortable and alive in the worship setting.

Such statements point out the power of ritual, those repetitious signs, symbols, sayings, or actions that promote verbal and nonverbal responses. While many of these are obvious, such as liturgy, the church calendar, Scripture reading, preaching, singing, and gathering, many are less obvious but equally important for the messages they share.

Our physical setting and surroundings tell people who we are, what we value, and what is important to us. Our worship folders or bulletins tell others what we see as central to the worship experience. Our greeting in the narthex defines and shapes what people will experience that day. Each member is a mirror that reflects the values important to the church.

The prayers, hymns, sacraments, and preaching during the service all send a message to the participants as to how the church views its relationship with God. It is these rituals, and others, that allow us to transcend the common and ordinary so that we might believe. It is a finite means for helping us touch the infinite.

What rituals are you involving people in at your church? What do strangers feel when they enter your parking lot, walk through your doors, or sit in your pews? Do they feel accepted and loved even before the worship begins? Are they perceived as fellow members of the body of Christ or a threat to a protected environment? The rituals we establish have a tremendous impact on making others feel comfortable worshiping and learning and growing in faith.

Rituals have an impact on how people encounter God. By focusing on how we involve each person before, during, and after the worship experience, we can express the inexpressible acts of God for each of those present.

Interpreting Your Rituals

What messages are your rituals conveying to members or nonmembers? It could help to take a look at the following:

1. Physical setting. What do the church surroundings say to visitors?

2. Printed material from the church. What are you saying in the literature you print and distribute?

3. Greeting visitors. Are your greeters warm and open? Do they exhibit attitudes representative of your church?

4. Conversations with members. What do members tell others about your church? Is it inviting?

5. Observe how people spend their time. Are people happy to spend time at church before and after the service, or do they suddenly disappear?

SECURITY

How to Improve Security at Your Church

Theft is on the increase at churches across the nation, but there are some simple things you can do to protect your church from crime.

1. Self-Assessment
Look at your church building through the eyes of a burglar. Do a self-assessment of your facility beginning at the front door and going around the entire building. If you were a burglar, what do you see as the easiest point of entry? Check doors and windows.

2. Police Assessment
Contact your local police department and ask them to assess your building and suggest ways to make it safer.

3. Outdoor Lighting
Are there any areas of the outside of the church that are dark at night and hidden from public view by bushes? Consider strategic outdoor lighting near doors and windows.

4. Good Locks
A dead bolt lock with a steel bar at least one-inch long is your best protection from burglary. A dead bolt lock on both the inside and outside of the door is safer still because it prevents a person from breaking glass in the door and reaching around and opening it from the inside. This also prevents a burglar from exiting through the door if original entry was from a window.

5. Solid Doors
Can any door of your church be kicked in? Doors need to be reinforced with steel or metal plates. Glass doors should have unbreakable safety glass.

6. Indoor Lights

Leave a light on in the church office at night and also in any open foyer areas. Make it look like someone is inside.

7. Internal Security

If a burglar entered your building, how many locked doors would he have to pass through before entering an area with valuables or money? Check how many obstacles you can place between a burglar and your valuables after entry to a building.

8. Windows

Make sure your windows are always locked from the inside. If the window is not a fire exit, drive a nail above it so that it cannot be opened more than five inches. If permitted by fire regulations, add steel bars to high risk windows.

9. Burglar Alarms

There are many effective burglar alarms on the market. Check with a firm regarding your specific needs. Some alarms have battery backups in case the power is cut. Others can also detect smoke and fire.

These are a few of the many things you can do to make sure your church is crime free. Crime happens because the opportunity is there. Don't give them the opportunity and your church will be a safer place.

VOLUNTEERS

Empowering Them Through Covenants

Ever considered creating written covenants for the volunteers who serve within your congregation? It's a real opportunity to empower your team toward greater personal and spiritual growth.

The dictionary defines a covenant as a "binding agreement made by two or more individuals to do or keep from doing a specified thing." In other words, it can be a set of guidelines for establishing the ground rules on how people are to accomplish a specified task. These guidelines can be applied to most volunteers within church ministry, including Sunday school teachers, council members, youth workers, and Bible study leaders—anyone who has leadership responsibilities.

Why go through all the work? To begin with, covenants show you expect a serious commitment from your volunteers. They also help clarify expectations in the areas of time and talent. Covenants can create a vision for ministry as well, even in areas such as behavioral expectations. They can help you obtain a terrific overview of your objectives for your volunteers, the church, and yourself. Covenants can be a valuable resource in future planning and evaluations, too.

You can begin the process by writing a ministry description. Elements of the description can include the role of the volunteer, responsibilities, gifts and talents desired, who the person reports to and works with, length of service, any training to be given, and how you will support the people involved.

Next, consider the type of qualities you would like your volunteers to possess as they perform their work. What traits are most important as they serve the people of your church? Here are some suggestions:

1. Honesty: To take risks in being open with others and to communicate feelings directly.

2. Love and Support: To love those being ministered to, affirming them as children of God.

3. Sensitivity: To be sensitive to others, their needs, and their circumstances.

4. Confidentiality: To respect information given in confidence and treat it as such.

5. Prayer: To personally use the power of prayer in ministry and to encourage others to do the same.

6. Availability: To give time, talent, and effort to participants as required for ongoing ministry.

7. Commitment: To serve for a specific length of time.

8. Accountability: To be accountable to you, those being served, to God, and to the church.

These are some of the qualities and expectations that deserve to be communicated as volunteers begin their work. It is appropriate to conclude this document with space for your signature as well as that of the volunteer.

Though writing a covenant won't eliminate all misunderstandings between you and your volunteers, it can provide a solid foundation from which to begin.

VOLUNTEERS

How to Get People to Do Things

At the turn of the century, a man placed this challenge in a London newspaper in the form of an advertisement: "Men wanted for hazardous journey. Small wages, bitter cold, long months of complete darkness, constant danger, safe return doubtful. Honor and recognition in case of success. . . ."

The response to the ad was so great, many were turned away. The advertiser was Sir Ernest Shackleton and his objective was to gather together a group of men to explore the Antarctic. He knew the secret of motivation was to challenge others. It's a principle that still works wonders today.

If you are looking for ways to motivate others, challenging them is one of many ways you can move others toward accomplishment. Certainly Christ challenged his followers, and centuries later their impact is still being made. If the challenge is presented in a positive manner and appeals to a dream or special interest, it can be a sure method of generating results.

Challenges work because they appeal to our sense of importance. People want to be involved in something that impacts others positively. "Honor and recognition in case of success" is a real motivator. And there is an almost uncontrollable urge to do things for a friend who makes us feel that we are special.

How can you harness this power in your congregation? It can be as simple as offering appreciation or taking the time to listen, then challenging your people in faith to act on their dreams. Remember, it's the little things that make a ministry effective.

VOLUNTEERS WANT TO HELP

For some reason, I always feel a little uncomfortable calling people to help. I think of their commitments, their other concerns, or their helping out of guilt rather than enjoyment. I also want to avoid burning out those faithful regulars who are at the church before you can hang up the phone. Somehow I feel as though I'm infringing on their private territory.

Studies have shown, however, that most people volunteer because they want to do something useful. They want to help out. One gentleman from our congregation was upset because he had signed up to help and was never called to serve. He not only felt rejected, but soon felt apathetic towards the church as a whole. His comments mirrored his frustration: "The church talks but never gets anything done." He wanted to help; he simply wasn't given the opportunity.

Others echoed his sentiments in ensuing conversations. They felt that the church was at its best when people joined together to help, whether it involves organizing a chicken dinner fund raiser or putting up a structure together. Helping was important to them, not only for the mission of the church, but also because it was a concrete act of faith.

In a national survey on "Giving and Volunteering in the United States," it was estimated that 45 percent of American adults volunteer. It also reported that those who volunteer tend to give twice as much to charity as those who do not volunteer. Those who didn't volunteer reported being "too busy."

Research done by the Institute for the Advancement of Health also showed positive benefits in helping. People relieved stress, learned coping skills, and built up their self-esteem. Many received a "runner's calm" from their altruistic activities.

Jesus' call to serve was not an idle remark to get the chores done. It is a way that we can call those around us to live out their faith in an important, immediate, and tangible way. Those who give of themselves find a reward that goes beyond the realms of this world.